**DO NOT REMOVE
CARDS FROM POCKET**

ALLEN COUNTY PUBLIC LIBRARY

FORT WAYNE, INDIANA 46802

You may return this book to any agency, branch,
or bookmobile of the Allen County Public Library.

DEMCO

The Headhunter Strategy

The Headhunter Strategy

How to Make It Work for You

KENNETH J. COLE

JOHN WILEY & SONS
New York • Chichester • Brisbane • Toronto • Singapore

Library of Congress Cataloging in Publication Data:

Cole, Kenneth J.
  The headhunter strategy.

  Includes index.
  1. Executives—Recruiting.   I. Title.

HD38.2.C645   1985   650.1'4'024658   84-27025
ISBN 0-471-81943-3

Printed in the United States of America

10 9 8 7 6 5 4 3 2 1

FOREWORD

Why are so many managers inept at marketing themselves and unwise or unrealistic in their career strategies? What economic tasks are performed by various kinds of recruitment, placement, and search firms? Why should individuals and companies have a close and continuing relationship with reputable and responsible headhunters? How does one uncover opportunities and pursue them effectively? These are a few of the questions addressed by Kenneth J. Cole in *The Headhunter Strategy*. In writing this book he has done a great service for both job seekers and people seekers in the managerial marketplace. He has produced a provocative and clear explanation of how the market for executive and managerial talent really works. He has stripped away much of the myth and mystique of the recruitment and search game.

In some ways this is the ultimate how-to-do-it book. He explains in detail how to organize and conduct a systematic job search and how to improve the odds of finding a better, more rewarding employment situation. He explains how to use recruit-ment and search professionals and how to avoid numerous pitfalls. But this is no superficial cookbook. It is a serious attempt to develop principles and to evaluate techniques. It is packed with information, source materials, insights, cogent analysis, and rare good sense. In a game where most of the players are amateurs, he provides first class professional advice in a lucid and lively manner.

Although much of the focus of the book is on the job candidate, there is sage advice for companies as well. The corporation trying to field the most effective managerial team should know how to use recruitment and search professionals—and even how to re-duce unnecessary and unwanted turnover in the managerial ranks.

I am not in the search or placement business but over the years in the course of my work as the Director of The Executive Program of the Graduate School of Business at The University of Chicago, I have watched hundreds of careers blossom and some go sour. I have talked with hundreds of executives about their career goals and strategies. *The Headhunter Strategy* will help me enormously, because I can say to them, "Read this book!" It will make them think, give them a realistic view of the market, and greatly increase their effectiveness in setting and pursuing their personal and professional goals. We are indebted to Ken Cole for his compulsion and his wisdom.

WALTER D. FACKLER
Director of The Executive Program
Graduate School of Business
The University of Chicago

PREFACE

Has putting off a project you knew you were *morally* responsible for ever kept you awake at night? Writing *The Headhunter Strategy*—or rather, months of putting it off—did that to me, until I finally "faced the music" and did it.

Why did I bother to write *THS* and why should you read it? *You are going to mismanage your job campaign without this book.* Other authors haven't told you the truth. "Popular" knowledge about headhunters is all twisted up. *The Headhunter Strategy* tells the *truth* about job campaigns. It will give you all the tools to put together an effective job campaign and manage your career after that.

In retrospect, procrastinating wasn't hard—like you, I have more things to do than hours in the day to do them. Organizing projects into available time wasn't the problem; I work as hard at that as anyone I know. Payoff was; I'm swimming upstream—fighting the body of "popular knowledge"—with much of the book. Recognition of that contributed to the delay. No matter: for those who choose to act on what is presented in *The Headhunter Strategy*, financial and responsibility upgrades will be greater and more frequent. I'm certain of it.

I wrote *The Headhunter Strategy* because it had to be done; too many executives mishandle contacts with headhunters. If you were able to manage these contacts more effectively, everyone would benefit: you, for financial and responsibility upgrades; corporations, to gain access to talent otherwise not found; headhunters, to fill more positions. (Did you realize that when a "headhunter" fills a positon, he or she pleases 75% of all involved parties? The individual gets the "new and better" position. The gaining employer hires the manager it was looking for. The headhunter earns a fee. The only "loser" is the "old" organization, and it's not always a "loser." Chances are about even that because the executive was being held back for some reason—any reason, it doesn't matter—the "loss" was timely. Also, the departure of any manager creates opportunities—sometimes a major chain reaction of promotions—for those lower in the organization's structure. That's healthy, one of the reasons turnover is expected, and is a strength of the system, not a weakness.)

The work that "headhunters" do is generally misunderstood by "civilians." Even headhunters won't agree on what they do; ask ten—you'll get ten different answers. Part of the difficulty in describing what the headhunter does springs from the fact that several very different processes are going on under the banners of "executive search," "personnel consulting," "recruiting," "executive marketing," "retained search," etc. No wonder everyone is confused.

"Headhunting" is a big business—bigger than you suspected. I have documented the existence of over 20,000 active firms in the United States. These companies vary in size from one person to a hundred (or more) recruiters, averaging about six recruiters per firm. Nationally, *recruiters fill over a million jobs per year* at levels from clerk to Chairman of the Board. Fees generated? $5 billion or more is a pretty good estimate of the dollar volume—extend the numbers yourself.

Why should you involve "headhunters" in your career strategy? Would you represent yourself in court? Would you drill and fill your own teeth? Or, can you determine your true worth within the "closed system" of your own organization? No, no, and no. A headhunter—a person who is a "third party" to the staffing function—will help optimize your value, to yourself, to your company, and to society.

A road map is a useful tool to prevent driving out of your way, isn't it? That thought also occurred to me one day as I was writing an article for the executive search business. So, we developed The Recruiting Model© to explain who does what in executive search. These approaches are outlined carefully. They are readily adaptable to your situation, and are as effective for CEO's as they are for midlevel managers. These strategies will provide a three-or four-stride lead over your competition in the 100-yard dash when a quick job change is necessary.

Over the long run, a very different strategy will be beneficial. Developing an effective relationship with an industry or functional "specialist" headhunter will help ensure that you will be considered for salary and responsibility upgrades to keep you rewarded and challenged to your potential. This is frequently impossible to achieve within your firm: Even the best-run and most progressive organization's system can become "backed-up" with effective and loyal managers who won't "look outside," but are capable of producing more for another organization, and, ultimately, themselves. Headhunters break this "logjam" by moving managers to organizations ready to recognize the individual's higher potential. As a free-market force, headhunters help reduce labor market inefficiencies that exist between corporations. *The Headhunter Strategy* will show you how to develop the "long-run" relationship, and suggest some ways it will be of major benefit to you.

There are side benefits to the long-term relationship as well. Headhunters are a valuable source of competitive information when managed correctly. They will tell you when you are compensating your employees competitively and help *you* reduce *your* firm's turnover. To obtain the benefits of the third-party staffing function, you simply have to understand it and plug into it.

I did not want to revolutionize the job-search process, but some of the techniques used for approaching "headhunters" are also useful for approaching potential employers. *The Headhunter Strategy* outlines how to "employ" those principles throughout your job search. *THS* is a *very* different sort of book. I believe it is the most pragmatic approach to executive-level job campaigning written. I promise you plenty of work, no foolishness, and an original approach. Good hunting!

KENNETH J. COLE

Panama City Beach, Florida
January 1985

CONTENTS

xi

PART 3   THE HEADHUNTER STRATEGY

The Headhunter Strategy

— PART **1**—

GROUNDWORK

— 1 —

The Resume Defrocked

Every book ever written on jobhunting or jobchanging has a section on resumes. It's often an important section, sometimes the major thrust of the book. Authors advise—in agonizing detail—what to say and what not. They advise on paper choice, typeface, printed versus typed versus photocopied. They rattle off advantages and disadvantages of "functional" and "chronological" formats. Blah, blah, blah . . . Phooey! The resume section is also an important part of this book—I've consciously spent a lot of time on it—but I hope to convince you that resumes are not useful, at least not for early contact with headhunters or potential employers.

Although "they" proffer plenty of advice on how to craft a "hard-hitting" resume, this is one time it pays *not* to listen to what "they" say. The resume is the classic "nonevent."

Not *one* of the books I have read on the subject (I've plowed through about a hundred and don't recommend this sort of project for anyone, unless you're masochistic or have an extremely high tolerance for pain) has demonstrated an understanding of what a resume (1) will do, or (2) won't do.

Did you ever wonder whether a resume—even a "perfect" resume—works, in the sense of *getting you hired*? I believe that resumes hurt more than help and there are alternatives.

Fact:	Resume-readers come in two basic categories—"scanners" and "pickers."
	The typical hiring manager is a "scanner." He hasn't been trained to read resumes, couldn't care less what sort of style you use (as long as there is plenty of "white space"), and more or less randomly skips around the document. Average reading time is *30 seconds*, with 80% of the reading effort devoted to the first page, the other 20% to all pages following. The scanner doesn't have a lot of time to devote to reading resumes and probably wouldn't spend very much time reading them if he or she had the time.
Conclusion:	If you have something to say, it had better be on the first page and it had better be obvious. Put it on page 2 (or later), and it probably won't be read.
Fact:	*Thorough* resume readers are "pickers." Fortunately for you, they are in the minority. They will spend *lots* of time on the resume, "picking" through every comment, looking for "knockout items"— *items that screen you out of consideration for the position, instead of considering reasons to hire you.*
Conclusion:	What you considered an honest summary of responsibilities, accomplishments, education,

and interests may work against you. This is one time when candor is destructive.

Fact: Resume exaggeration—even outright lying —is rampant; even at executive levels. (A common observation in the search business is that Harvard Business School gets "credit" for five or six times as many graduates as it ever had.) Tom Norton, President of FideliFacts, a major reference checking and credential verification service, estimates that as many as 30% of all resumes contain exaggerations, blatant lies, or accomplishments that cannot be supported by checking the candidate's background.

Conclusion: *In the resume format,* much of what you say isn't going to be believed. The *most* a resume can do is keep you under consideration for the position. That's a *very* weak positive when you consider the resume will either be skimmed, scrutinized for the wrong reasons, or dismissed.

So, a resume *may* be read, *can* screen you out, and *may* be believed. It *will not* get you the position you want: only a series of interviews can do that. By all means, write your resume, but *don't* send it to anyone (headhunters, potential employers, blind ads, etc.) *yet.* (We'll come back to what to do with it at the right time.) In any event, resume writing is a very beneficial exercise in self-assessment you should undertake *every year.* Keeping your resume current by charting what you have accomplished and how you did it is an important part of tracking your progress.

Write a resume, but don't send it? That sounds like heresy. How could anything else work any better or at all?

The explanation is simple, straightforward, and compelling:

Resumes contain too much information, information that isn't relevant, information that distracts the reader, and disinformation. In short, information overload, which can cause too many bad things to happen.

If resume readers were universally competent at evaluating your potential contributions to the firm or to the client based on what you say about yourself (unfortunately, they are not), resumes might be useful. But line managers *are not good at evaluating resumes.* Personnel people are even worse. They tend to toss out good ones with bad ones for factors irrelevant to job performance. Headhunters are a little better, but not much.

Regardless of what I say and no matter how persuasive my position is, you may decide to broadcast-mail your resume. If you do, here are the gross mistakes that cause bad things to happen (and why). This isn't intended as an all-inclusive "laundry list" of everything that can be screwed up, but it's a lot of them.

Mistakes of Form

1. Longer than two pages. Candidate has an unrealistic view of own importance; even Lee Iacocca, Frank Borman, and Ronald Reagan could write hard-hitting two-pagers. Or, candidate is weak in prioritizing/organizing skills. Accomplishments are lost forever when they are buried and can't be found in a multipage epistle.

2. Cutesy. Off-size paper, fluorescent colors, "Olde English" print, and so on. You name it, someone has tried it. Candidate is instantly judged to be naive and unprofessional. Or, send it bound as a book, in a presentation folder, or include a title page with name and address. If headhunters and line managers saved all this stuff, the office would soon be stacked solid. (I give the presentation folders to my kids for book reports).

3. Printing a photograph as part of the resume or including one. Candidate is judged narcissistic or is suspected to have sent a picture of someone else. Photos totally eliminate an objective review of the document and are major distractions.

4. Typesetting. Implies you are desperate and mailing thousands. Headhunters don't like distressed goods—even those dressed up in fancy packages. Save the typesetting/printing expense and invest those dollars in word processing at the local secretarial service.

5. Photocopies. Implies you can't afford typesetting or didn't think of it.

6. Grammatical errors, typos, erasures, misspelled words, or typed on the Smith-Corona Aunt Sally left you in her will. Again, candidate is written off as unprofessional.

7. Don't ever call your resume a c.v. ("curriculum vitae," which I gather is Latin for resume), unless you're a health professional (MD, DO, DDS, etc.) or an academic; then, it's acceptable. Even if you're not one, the headhunter will label you a pointy-headed academic.

Mistakes of Substance

1. Falsification of credentials. There are more ways to do this than space to list them; all can be checked, and increasingly, are. Major employers are extensively using third-party firms to check candidate backgrounds: Firms such as National Credential Verification Service, Fidelifacts, Proudfoot, and others specialize in substantiating candidate backgrounds and uncovering lies. Resume lying is grounds for later dismissal, regardless of performance. This creates even bigger problems and is not worth the risk.

2. Rambling, flowery descriptions of past and present duties that give no clue of what was accomplished or how. Employers and headhunters are impressed with *accomplishments* described by active-voice verbs and numbers: "Increased profits by $3 million by eliminating unprofitable lines;" "Directed reorganization of the data processing department, eliminating three programmers (annual savings of $178,000) and increasing output of department by 20%;" "Reduced manufacturing scrap rate by 47 tons per shift through rebuild of the #3 crusher—annual profit improvement, $18 million;" "Negotiated 5-year contract with UAW, eliminating COLA provisions and placing 4% cap on annual increases, saving $9 million in direct labor costs," and so forth.

3. Be careful about including "memberships" and "accomplishments" that work in reverse. American Management Association membership carries slightly less weight with headhunters than does membership in the National Geographic Society. When you include this sort of "credential" on your resume, you get snickers and "B" status (more on that in Chapter 5), not serious consideration.

RESUMES, RESUMES, EVERYWHERE RESUMES

I suspect that more hours have been spent writing, crafting, drafting, and revising resumes than went into building the pyramids. Enough copies have been printed to fill the Library of Congress several times. Resume gurus earn their livings creating resumes for job seekers at *fees of up to a thousand dollars!* (Not bad for a day's work or less.) They'll even do it over the phone (on your nickel and charged to your favorite credit card).

Like most headhunters, I get lots of unsolicited resumes and rarely read them. I do keep a "rogues' gallery" of favorites—only the *truly* awful ones qualify for this honor—that go up on the bulletin board. My all-time favorite (you would have to see this one to believe it):

Nine pages, three colors of paper, a mixture of typesetting and a personal computer printer.

Includes a test to take at the end to check my comprehension of the material.

Includes important data such as all the magazines the candidate subscribes to, education since elementary school, 16 references to contact for additional information, a list of the 26 seminars attended over the 14-year period he had 9 different jobs.

A full-color picture of the smiling candidate in cardigan sweater and tie.

This one is remarkable—I continue to marvel at it every time I look at it and wonder what sort of results he obtained from his job campaign.

By using the contact methods outlined in *THS*, you won't need more than a dozen or so resumes, so don't waste money having them printed.

Debating the use (or nonuse) of the resume is a little like debating theology; you can score points, but creating converts is a low-percentage proposition. If you press your position too hard, you can even turn friends against you. While aware of that, I still hope to convince you there is a better way to present yourself to employers and headhunters than by using resumes.

Here's the first step toward contacting potential employers and headhunters. Assemble these documents:

☐ All notes you have ever used to prepare for personal performance reviews.

☐ All written performance reviews and critiques provided for you by past supervisors.

☐ All resumes used in previous job campaigns plus the resume you planned to use for this one. (But don't bother to write a new one if you have not.)

Now, using these documents as inspiration (add other details as they come into your head), select the eight or ten *most significant accomplishments* of your business career. Write down what you did, how you did it, how your firm benefited (preferably in dollars earned or saved), and how/why you could repeat this performance at another organization.

This exercise should fill three or four pages on a legal pad. (If you use up the whole legal pad, read the directions again. This isn't intended to be the unabridged history of your business career). Now, *using a strict one-page limit*, edit these *accomplishments* down to the *four or five best*.

Save your resume for followup after contacts have been made and interviews are in progress—you're going to need the accomplishments sheet first. We'll show you what to do with it in Chapter 10.

Headhunters and hiring managers *really do want to hear from attractive candidates*. The headhunter earns fees by bringing superior candidates to the client. The hiring manager wants superior candidates from the headhunter and attempts to make good hires alone as well. But, *headhunters and hiring managers will brutally attack the information you send them*. Do yourself a favor and *don't send resumes*. If you must be screened out of consideration, make certain it happens on a telephone or personal interview, not from a "pick" or "scan" of your resume.

Later in *The Headhunter Strategy* we'll go step-by-step through a method much stronger than a bare resume, or resume with a "cover letter" (another favorite strategy "they" suggest). This method will create more contacts, stronger headhunter and line manager interest in your background, help you manage followup contact and interviews, and stretch you limited job campaigning dollars farther. First, let's examine third-party staffing and consulting and put some order into a business that appears confusing and cluttered.

= 2 =

Who—and What—
Is a Headhunter?

You've heard many of the names: executive recruiter, flesh-peddler, body snatcher, employment agency, management adviser, personnel consultant, human resource adviser, outplacement executive. How about: retained search, contingent search, consultant to management on executive selection, consultant in organizational human resource management (wow!), executive marketer, and just plain headhunter? There are so many other names being used that cataloging all of them would be difficult.

To complicate the issue a little more—CPA's often have side-line search departments. Management consultants dabble in it. Even a few ad agencies get into the act by acting as "resume drops" for their clients.

The headhunting "profession" (if you group everything going on in this business and put it under one umbrella) has a checkered reputation. Like most businesses, it has shady operators. They have managed to paint the whole business one nefarious color. Whenever a weak "headhunter" or flim-flam artist succeeds in passing himself (herself) off as something he (she) is not, it hurts the entire industry and adds to the confusion. There is plenty of that going on.

By now, I hope you have concluded the firm's name isn't very useful in determining what it does. We'll spend this chapter (and the next one) examining the "headhunting" business. Then, if you have decided to conduct a job campaign, I'll show you how to make it more effective, and optimize the progression of your career by developing relationships with recruiters.

For a minute, forget everything you know (or think you know) about headhunters and we'll start with a clean slate.

First, several definitions:

Headhunter. A third party to the employment or staffing process, who earns his (her) fee by performing employment or staffing services for corporations (or other firms or organizations) or individuals.

Headhunters perform two basic services (only two):

1. Pure Recruiting. The headhunter starts with a qualification list ("wish list") provided by a client, then locates and attracts the candidate(s) best meeting the list of qualifications.

2. Candidate Marketing. The headhunter starts with a candidate, and fits him (her) into a position with a client he (she) is best qualified to fill.

Fees headhunters earn come in two varieties (only two):

1. Retained Fees. The headhunter is paid on a progress basis like any other consultant or like a contractor building a house.
2. Contingent Fees. The headhunter is paid when the assignment is completed successfully. If no hire is made, the headhunter earns no fee.

Boiled down to the basics, that's what a headhunter does—anything else is secondary.

These definitions can be used to describe every headhunter in the business, from Acme Employment Agency of Biloxi to the firm with the thickest carpets on the highest floor of the tallest building in Manhattan. Every one. And there are lots of them in business.

We estimate there are over 20,000 "headhunting" firms in the United States, averaging about six headhunters each. Even if you want to quarrel with the numbers, there are plenty to go around with headhunters in every state. While every state has at least a few firms, they are centered around the major business communities of New York, Chicago, Los Angeles, and Houston. (In fact, on my mailing list of over 11,000 firms, fully half are in the states of New York, Illinois, California, and Texas.) Every business form, from sole proprietorship to public corporation, is represented. Overall, though, it's a collection of small businesses run by entrepreneurs. Remember that; you'll need it later in the book.

Now it starts getting a little more cluttered.

☐   All levels of expertise, from no expertise to excellence, are represented.

What does it take to become a "headhunter"? A telephone, a desk, and a business card will do it. While states have regulated, reregulated, and deregulated the "agency" business (where individual candidates, not corporate clients, pay the headhunters' fees), "executive search" firms generally fall through the regulatory cracks. The definition of an "executive search firm" in Illinois (an operation that fills no positions at salaries *under* $15,000 per year and accepts no fees from candidates) is typical. So, it's an easy business to enter, and as such, attracts many people, at all levels of skill, driven by the lure of "giant fees" to be earned.

☐   There are no nationally recognized credentials or standards for "headhunters" to be measured against.

That's not entirely true; there are two. Membership in the Association of Executive Search Consultants (AESC) carries a lot of prestige. This is the "upper crust" (or a part of the upper crust) of the search business, but there are only 55 member firms. While membership is restricted to retained firms only, many prestigious retained firms are *not* members. Membership is expensive, plus there is a fair amount of backbiting that goes on between the members. AESC members fill many senior-level positions, but so do nonmembers.

At the other end of the scale is the Certified Personnel Consultant (CPC) designation, awarded by the National Association of Personnel Consultants (NAPC). To receive the CPC designation, a recruiter must complete a course of instruction (on state regulations, EEO laws, business ethics, interviewing skills, etc.), take a test (administered by the state association), and have 2 years' experience in the business. NAPC has awarded about 4500 CPCs since 1960. We'll give them high marks for initiative, but unfortunately, the CPC designation carries little weight. (Had you heard of it before I told you? PR efforts are not NAPC's strong suit.)

Although both the top and bottom ends of the scale are "self-regulated," AESC and NAPC memberships require acceptance of "ethical" principles. This leaves the other 90% of the business operating on conscience and (more or less) within the law. Considering the size of this group, expect an equally wide range of "ethics."

SELECTING A HEADHUNTER

Make a separate decision about each headhunter before considering an alliance (see Chapters 14 and 15). Because the "market" for recruiting services cleans out nonperformers fairly quickly, tenure in the business is a decent indicator of the individual recruiter's abilities. If a recruiter has been around for 3 or 4 years, through the good times and bad times of a complete business cycle, he or she is a survivor.

Turnover is a major concern in the recruiting business: 90% or more of the rookies don't make it. In the second year, half of the 10% surviving the first year will drop out. In following years, turnover drops dramatically, and resembles that of most other businesses—5% or so per year.

Returning to the confusion issue: because many recruiters—beginners, mainly—equate strong selling skills with recruiting capability, there is a perpetual scramble for higher-paying assignments, with recruiters taking on more assignments than can be performed and making overblown promises to clients. Firms specializing in lower and midlevel assignments aren't the only offenders, though. Some of the "top tier" retainer-only firms have also lost the recruiting edge. Why bother to recruit when notoriety delivers a tidal wave of resumes (from some very fine managers) to bank in a computerized data base?

Some of the best recruiting (and candidate marketing) is produced by solo operators and small partnerships. Public profiles of many of these firms are low, so don't be concerned if you don't know the name.

Because we're concentrating on your *personal* relationship with recruiters, we'll brush by the subject of selecting search firms for filling your firm's vacancies except for several quick points:

☐   The firm's recruiting capabilities are more important than thick carpets and forty-seventh floor locations in midtown. Get references from past satisfied clients and check them.

☐   Be certain you know who will be handling your assignment. Beware of "front men" turning assignments over to junior researchers.

☐   Recruiters overestimate their abilities to complete a given assignment about as often as clients overestimate the amount of recruiter horsepower required. Pick the recruiter appropriate to the job.

TO RETAIN OR NOT TO RETAIN

You have undoubtedly read somewhere that the retained relation-·ship between corporate clients and executive recruiter is "better." There is no question that the major retained firms have worked hard to foster that image (they have) and that retained work is better for the recruiter. By eliminating contingent fees, the client bears all the risk. (Under the contingent arrangement, the recruiter gets the fee only if the position is filled.)

The theory behind the retained relationship is that the recruiter is compensated for professional services rendered as they are performed. But are they really performed if no hire is consummated?

There's no question that *work* is performed, but the work has little value to the client in the absence of a hire. The major retained firms like to compare their services to those of the distinguished surgeon, whose fees are payable even when the patient dies on the operating table (after all, the operation *was* successful). And they pooh-pooh the value of contingent work (e.g., AESC membership rules prohibit contingent fees, although industry talk says the rule is regularly winked at). Despite the fact that many other professionals (attorneys, real estate brokers, etc.) earn handsome livings through quality contingent work.

Another fallacy is that because of the retained relationship, the major retained firms can be more selective of candidates, so their loyalties are with their clients. Let's clear the air once and for all on these points (remember, you read it in *THS*):

☐   Recruiting is a business, not missionary work. The recruiter's first loyalty is to himself, not clients, not candidates.

☐   Success or failure in recruiting is a function of how effectively candidates are attracted and hired, not how the firm is compensated. Some of the best recruiters in the country are 100% contingent because they prefer to work that way.

☐   The major retained firms have seized the attention of the business press and the notoriety that brings—but not the major share of recruiting. Most recruiting is contingent and is performed for midlevel, *not* top-level, positions. I estimate that 80% of all search work (measured by fees generated) is performed to fill positions with salary levels of $30,000–75,000 per year. These are *not* the positions making headline news.

☐   Don't be confused about what recruiters do—they fill positions for a fee.

Our next chapter will make you an expert on headhunters.

— 3 —

The Recruiting Model

I read somewhere once that the average person is lucky to have a handful of truly original thoughts in a lifetime. I stumbled onto one several years ago while writing my newsletter "The Recruiting & Search Report" for the executive search community. The basic idea developed into *The Recruiting Model*, now widely recognized as a useful tool to understand third-party recruiting work. It should be useful in your job campaign as well and later in your executive role when you are selecting third-party staffing assistance.

Four basic varieties of firms are involved in third-party staffing work. They may go by a hundred or so different names, but there are only four ways to go about work as a headhunter:

1. Outplacement Organizations. They accept money from individuals ("private" outplacement) or from corporations sponsoring individuals ("corporate" outplacement) to

conduct job campaigns for displaced employees. The fee is paid up front (retained fees) and the firm "markets" the individual (candidate marketing).

2. Employment Agencies. Working primarily with candidates who "find them" by some means, they market the candidates to employers that can potentially use their skills. Fees are earned either from the candidate ("Applicant Paid Fees") or the employer ("Employer Paid Fees"), but only after the candidate is successfully "placed" in a position (contingent fees).

3. Contingent Search Firms. Instead of depending on "walk-in" or "mail-in" candidates, they "custom locate" (recruit) candidates for their corporate clients and are paid on successful assignment completion (contingent fees).

4. Retained Search Firms. Like contingent search firms, retained search firms custom locate candidates (recruit), but they are paid up front, or on a progress basis (retained fees).

There is virtually nothing else to do in third-party staffing, boiled down to the basics, unless you start adding duties unrelated to headhunting. While considering and comparing the four different kinds of firms—what they do and how they are paid—I noticed some interesting relationships and started drawing pictures.

Outplacement firms and retained search firms resemble each other in the way they earn fees. Both are paid up front. Outplacement and retained search firms are different from agencies and contingent search firms, which earn contingent fees.

The situation flip-flops though when you compare the activities of the four types of firms. Outplacement firms do the same thing that agencies do: They "market" candidates. Retained search firms and contingent search firms both recruit candidates.

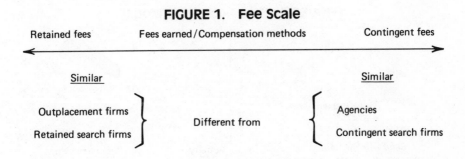

FIGURE 1.   Fee Scale

Retained fees   Fees earned/Compensation methods   Contingent fees

Similar   Similar

Outplacement firms   Agencies
                              Different from
Retained search firms   Contingent search firms

Then, the situation crystallized. The two scales in Figures 1 and 2 representing the firm's activity and how it is compensated can be used to define and explain all third-party staffing work. Lay the two scales together at right angles, and you create a very useful "map" of the business. This is *The Recruiting Model©* (Figure 3—a concept copyrighted by "The Recruiting & Search Report" newsletter).

Because the marketplace supports plenty of firms in each category, it's safe to assume each variety of headhunter is doing something right. (If the category of firm produced no value in the marketplace, all firms of that type would disappear.) Corporations select one type of firm over the other three types, depending on what sort of staffing problem the firm has.

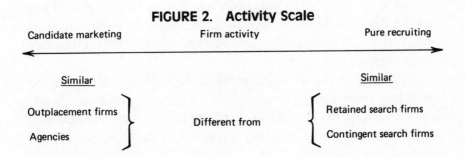

FIGURE 2.   Activity Scale

Candidate marketing   Firm activity   Pure recruiting

Similar   Similar

Outplacement firms   Retained search firms
                        Different from
Agencies   Contingent search firms

FIGURE 3.   The Recruiting Model

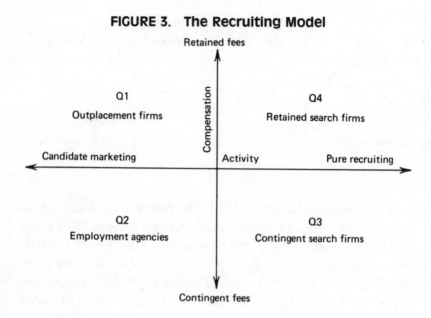

From this point on, we'll be referring to each category of firm by its quadrant location, abbreviated Q1, Q2, Q3 or Q4. For example, a Q2 firm markets candidates and is paid contingent fees. Q2 tells you more about the firm than employment agency (that title tells neither what the firm does nor how it is compensated); just remember the activity and compensation scales. (Really, this isn't complicated. Take another look at the picture.)

Consider the client's point of view: Each category of firm has advantages and disadvantages associated with its use for a staffing project. The major advantages and disadvantages for each type of firm are listed in Figure 4.

Corporate recruiters, personnel executives, and hiring managers face these considerations each time outside recruiting assistance is necessary. In addition (without even referring to how well a particular recruiter does his job), consider the facts that (1) few

Figure 4. Advantages and Disadvantages to Client

Advantages to Client	Disadvantages to Client
Q1 1. No fee exposure in most cases, even with successful hires; fee prepaid by "losing" employer or by the candidate. 2. Major Q1 firms often national in scope; large candidate base owing to overall state of economy and head-count reductions in many industries.	1. Candidate liabilities can be hidden by aggressive third-party marketing efforts. 2. Management time-investment necessarily high; heavy screening often required. 3. Candidates under consideration generally have been terminated by last employer; best candidates (those gainfully employed) excluded from consideration. 4. Loyalties of the Q1 firm to its candidates are superior to its loyalties to the potential employer.
Q2 1. Fee exposure strictly contingent upon successful hires. 2. Local (or regional) or industry candidate contacts of the Q2 firm are often extensive; may be additionally expanded through networking/multioffice operations.	1. Same as Q1. 2. Same as Q1. 3. Some terminated candidates (see 3 above), others are looking because of problems with present employer; candidates limited to these two groups. 4. Loyalties of Q2 recruiting firms often are split among multiple clients. 5. Firm undertakes multiple projects because of

Figure 4. (Continued)

Advantages to Client	Disadvantages to Client
	high-risk low percentage completion nature of business.
Q3 1. Same as Q2. 2. Same as Q2. 3. Loyalties of Q3 firm are with the client, not the candidate. 4. "Best" candidates are sought for the vacancy; most are gainfully employed.	1. Same as 5 in Q2. 2. Once an adequate candidate is located Q3 firm stops recruiting, presses for completion, or moves on to another assignment.
Q4 1. Same as 3 in Q3. 2. Same as 4 in Q3. 3. Dedicated effort on assignment.	1. Certain fee exposure, regardless of assignment completion. 2. Client has a vested interest in accepting work because of retained relationship. 3. Work on assignment limited to one recruiting firm; candidate access may therefore be limited.

recruiting firms understand these considerations above an instinctive level and (2) few fit the model in a "pure" sense (i.e. they move from quadrant to quadrant occasionally), and you will begin to understand the confusion in the marketplace over what it is that recruiters do.

Client expectations of the benefits to be derived from the recruiter's services vary widely, but the following expectations are commonly held by all corporations using recruiters:

The client expects the outside recruiter to save time and effort, and, therefore, money. It is less expensive to hire outside recruiting assistance than it is to perform all staffing activities internally. Recruiter fees are substantial, no question. Could the same work be duplicated internally at the same cost or for less? If the answer were yes, there would be no recruiting firms—all work would be done internally.

☐ The client expects the outside recruiter to provide access to candidates otherwise inaccessible. Any recruiter's success is a function of the strength of his or her contacts, contact loyalty, and where those contacts lead on any assignment. The client looks for "well-connected" recruiters and avoids those who cannot deliver hard-to-find candidates.

☐ The client expects the outside recruiter to understand its hiring needs and to present qualified candidates for consideration (qualified according to client standards, not recruiter standards).

☐ The client expects that recruiter conduct with the public will not reflect unfavorably on the client firm.

Take another look at the relative advantages and disadvantages in each quadrant. Even though each category is theoretically capable of successfully completing any assignment, it should be obvious to client and recruiter that recruiter selection is judgmental: The Acme Employment Agency is unlikely to be able to locate and bring about the successful hire of a Fortune 500 divisional general manager. But, the well-known retainer-only firm is just as unlikely to be able to locate a junior secretary in Biloxi, Mississippi. Different jobs require different staffing tactics.

Recruiters often overestimate their capabilities; clients overestimate their recruiting needs just as often. The reverse is also often true for both: Just as the recruiter may expend time and effort on assignments that aren't worth the trouble because they do not require his(her) particular strengths, client firms may select underpowered recruiters for assignments beyond the recruiter's capability. Again, recruiters and client firms must work hard at picking each other. Poor recruiter/client selection is a major cause of many frustrations and disappointments surrounding the search business.

Back to your role as a client of the recruiter. How do you know what sort of recruiter you are dealing with when you are approached? Consider these indicators:

1. Q1's are often effective at camouflage; since they often orchestrate a candidate's job search behind the scenes, you may not be aware of their existence. One clue is a resume too slick for a candidate's background. These become easier to detect once you have received several from the same source. Q1 firms are masters of hype. Their candidates are nearly always either unemployed or in the process of being terminated.

2. Q2's will approach clients with "perfect" candidates, often described as such before any vacancies have even been discussed or described. Or, the "recruiter" will produce an instant candidate for your vacancy. Interestingly, the Q2's fee schedule is often negotiable. (You get what you pay for?) Emphasis is on the quick fix; the "recruiter" has got a

lot of projects going. Also, the majority of Q2 candidates will be unemployed, "looking for greater challenges," or otherwise motivated to make a change. Remember, the candidate sought out the Q2 firm, not the other way around. The loyalty of the Q2 to any given candidate is unpredictable, because candidates are expendable; the Q2 has another "perfect" candidate to replace the rejected one, until someone tires of the process.

3. Q3's will resist pressure for quick solutions and will ask lots of questions—often sensitive ones and possibly more than you are used to answering. The Q3 recruiter will be stingy with candidates; they are hard to replace. The Q3 recruiter also will tend to be conspicuously absent after several candidates have been rejected. Expect resistance to fee negotiating. Q3's are often hostile to personnel people.

4. Q4's are the champion name-droppers and buzzword artists. They often prefer thick carpets and 42nd floor offices. While they'll probably be able to tell you who your competitors are and what your earnings per share were last year, knowledge of your industry may be superficial (few Q4's specialize in an industry or function; they prefer to be "generalists"). Expect self-serving descriptions of recruiter credentials, elaborate proposals, patronizing attitudes toward personnel people, and a very sharp "front man," who presents the proposal.

Figure 5 provides more data that should enhance your understanding of headhunters in terms of how they relate to each other in compensation ranges. (Ranges are approximate and designed to illustrate general relationships of each quadrant firm.)

This figure should help explain some of the marketplace confusion and a lot of the backbiting: Every variety of firm encroaches

FIGURE 5. Quadrant Relationships

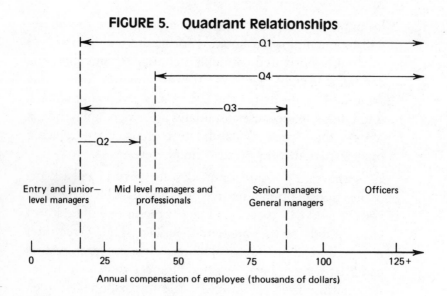

Annual compensation of employee (thousands of dollars)

on the edges of the others with one exception: Q2's don't compete with Q4's. This explains their relationship: Q2's look at Q4's with awe; Q4's look at Q2's with disdain. Otherwise, they are all competitors, and spend a fair amount of time and energy bad-mouthing each other.

While there are undoubtedly at least a few firms of each type working outside the normal salary parameters—Q2's specializing in "marketing" general managers and officer level candidates, or Q4's performing retained searches for clerks, and so on—it's a pretty safe bet that these are in the minority. So, at this point you can make some basic decisions concerning your job campaign: which variety (or varieties) of firms are likely to be most useful as contacts? Here is Figure 5 restated by organizational level and salary expectations. Use these data to help determine the categories of recruiters to contact:

Level	Salary Expectations	Contact
Entry/junior executive	to 25,000 ($\pm$)	Q2's, Q3's
Mid level	25,000–35,000 ($\pm$)	Q2's, Q3's
Mid level	35,000–70,000 ($\pm$)	Q3's, Q4's
Senior/General Managers	65,000–100,000 ($\pm$)	Q3's, Q4's
Officers	90,000–up	Q4's

Now you are an expert on headhunters. The information in this chapter will be useful in your job campaign, in selecting staffing assistance for your organization, and in developing long-term alliances with headhunters to optimize your personal career strategies.

— 4 —

When It's Time to Look

If you wrapped this book in a *Wall Street Journal* when you brought it home so no one would suspect the subject, don't feel guilty about it. A prospective employment change is one of the most stressful endeavors of your adult life. Wanting to keep the project private for a while isn't unusual. But enlisting an ally will be important later and this chapter will help when, at some point, you decide to share it with your spouse or close friend.

The U.S. economy is moving through a period of revolutionary changes. Important segments of the economy are shrinking and will *never* regain their former luster. They may never again offer the opportunities for personal growth they once did. Make no mistake about this—regardless of what you may or may not accomplish for your organization, it may never be capable of rewarding you for your accomplishments or challenging you to your capability. Declining markets, uncompetitive processes, foreign competition, interest rates, unfunded pension liabilities, changing consumer preferences; these and a thousand other factors can handcuff the future of your organization and even its larger industry.

An understanding of the underlying economic changes taking place is important to any manager, but particularly to those aspiring to general management or officer-level positions. Put these books on your mandatory reading list:

Economic Report of the President. Published annually (February) by the President's Council of Economic Advisers. The annual report is a public document required by law (Employment Act of 1946; amended by the Full Employment and Balanced Growth Act of 1978). Except for the politicized introduction added after the council transmits the document to the President, the book is apolitical. Economic developments of the past several years are followed by a forecast of what's coming, then another hundred pages or so of very useful statistics. You won't find this one in the bookstore so order book No. 040-000-0476-9 from Superintendent of Documents, U.S.G.P.O., Washington, DC 20402 ($8), or request a copy from your representative or senator (each receives "free" copies).

Megatrends (Naisbitt; Warner Books, 1982) and *The Third Wave* (Toffler; William Morrow & Co., 1980). Both books deal with the fundamental changes taking place in U.S. and world economies. *Megatrends* is more populist and easier to read. *The Third Wave* is heavier and a little flaky at times, but both are excellent and worth your time. Either may suggest new directions to take your career. Both are available in paperback editions as well; try any major bookstore.

So, regardless of your past contributions, future potential, or present loyalty, your firm and its industry may not be an attractive place to work anymore.

How did you associate with your organization anyway? Most managers—even senior executives—arrived through combinations of luck and timing rather than purpose. You saw an opportunity and grabbed it. But a lot of water has flowed under the bridge since. Would you make the same decision today? Very few careers are *started* with mature decisions; even when they are, circumstances can change dramatically.

I am an active recruiter for one group of U.S. manufacturers. (If you are in "my" industry, you know me. If you are not, you won't. Please don't send resumes.) As I look at my clients—and at those companies I consider sources—here is what I see:

☐ The dramatic growth rates and associated rapid promotion rates of the 1960's and early 1970's have slowed, and, in many organizations, have reversed direction.

☐ Organizations are "backed up" with promotable managers —managers ready for greater responsibilities and challenges and the financial rewards that follow—who are not getting the opportunities.

☐ *Every* major firm rewards and promotes *some* managers unworthy of the privilege. *Every* major firm *fails to* reward and promote *some* managers who should be rewarded and promoted.

☐ The *character and direction* of the firm "trickle down" from the senior executive. Changes in top management bring changes in the character and direction of the firm—and these changes may not be to your liking.

You may be a candidate to "look" (to determine what your services might be worth to another firm, whether you are being challenged to your capability, and if future returns of both of these might be greater by leaving rather than staying) if—

☐   The company or the industry is going nowhere or the future looks flat. For example, plants are closing, profits are squeezed, processes are no longer competitive, or industry capacity is underutilized.

For every industry in decline, there is another with a bright future. The best way to beat a sluggish system may be to leave it behind you.

☐   You made a political mistake or aligned yourself with a boss who made a political mistake.

Political mistakes are often remembered longer than performance mistakes. Starting over with another firm at a level equal to or greater than your current level with no political liabilities may pay big dividends.

☐   You are well-trained and performing well in an excellent organization.

By moving to an organization with less talent, or one not as well-run, opportunities to make a *significant* contribution may be considerably greater. If you have a choice, always take over a position that someone screwed up rather than one that was well run.

☐   You entered an organization at a level much lower than you now occupy, or

☐   You are convinced that you have abilities (and are qualified) to perform well in a position considerably higher than the one you now occupy.

Human nature being what it is, "good old Charlie" at Company A may remain "good old Charlie" much longer than necessary. With a company change, he becomes "Mr. Charles Jones, Esquire" at Company B and is not bound by who he once was, or how far he came, how fast. This is a critical issue, particularly when you consider that fresh "talent" is important in the growth strategies of many firms.

The bottom line of all of this is that you need not apologize to *anyone* for wanting to "look outside" the organization. In fact, you should be apologizing to yourself for lingering in an organization when you should be "looking."

I am convinced that *on the average*, the executive making several well-timed company changes will be rewarded—financially, and with greater responsibilities and both earned at a faster rate—than the equally qualified executive who "stays put."

WHERE WERE YOU WHEN I NEEDED YOU?

It has happened to me a hundred times. Six months after I approached an attractive candidate—and was brushed off—the phone rings. "Ken, my division has been sold. What can you do for me?" Not much; the job I was recruiting for is now filled; he's now a "B" candidate (more on that in the next chapter); in my eyes his judgment is suspect because *he wasn't even willing to listen to me* before.

Beware—very wary—of what headhunters consider to be unreasonable loyalties. The loyalties you feel toward your firm are rarely as strong in reverse. Even the strongest legs crumple quickly when blind-sided.

"Headcount reductions" are coming more and more frequently as our manufacturing economy evolves. Have you heard the expression "cutting down the trees and saving the monkeys"? Don't underestimate the possibility that when the time comes for the company to make a choice, your assistant will stay and you'll be excess. It happens every day to managers who believed it could not happen.

Changes in senior management are *almost certain* to generate turnover below if for no other reason than to bring in more familiar subordinates. Competent, loyal (and unprepared) managers are easily swept away as a result of top-level personnel changes.

Even leveraged buy-outs (LBOs) by existing management can jeopardize a fine executive's standing; LBOs by outsiders almost certainly will. One of the first tasks of any LBO group is to drive down the fixed costs that encouraged previous owners to sell. That translates into head-count reductions, usually deep ones. LBOs are increasingly popular—you'll find one or more discussed almost every day in *The Wall Street Journal*—as major corporations continue to redeploy assets and divisional managers get the chance to test entrepreneurial wings.

Don't expect early warning, either. If you are "on the way out," that is, if the corporation has decided to replace you, you may not find out about it until your replacement is hired. As a headhunter, one of my important duties has been to locate replacements for incumbent managers without their knowledge. I have frequently been instructed and informed, "We must keep this from John

Smith until his replacement is hired. We can't have him distracted from the job by a job campaign." Remember what I have said about the double standard for loyalty. If your CEO had to, he would eliminate one person at a time—you included—until the headcount was "1."

When you find yourself *forced* to conduct a job campaign, you lose *the single most important element* of an effective one: The *time* to conduct it effectively. Panic-driven job campaigns generally do not yield the results of well-planned and executed campaigns.

Measuring your value "in the marketplace" *does not* mean that you must solicit offers from other firms, circulate resumes, or otherwise jeopardize your current position. Because recruiters specializing in your industry or functional area have an excellent sense of "the market" for executives with comparable educations, experience, and responsibilities, they can give you an accurate estimate of what you *should* be earning, by comparisons with your contemporaries.

There is an identifiable total reward rate (present/future total compensation, responsibilities, perquisites, etc.) for executives at your level. Because the recruiter is a *disinterested third party* (see Chapter 14), the recruiter's opinion is, by definition, better than yours or your management's. All this provides you with little or no help, though, unless you are "plugged in" to a headhunter's system. I'll show you how to do that later in the book.

— 5 —

"A's" Versus "B's"

Here's another classification system. Bear with me; this one is more straightforward than The Recruiting Model©. Both are important, but if you are going to remember only one, make it this one. It will help to increase the "punch" of all aspects of your job campaign.

Divide the world into two groups of people: "A's" and "B's." The "A" group includes all the people *not* actively seeking an employment change. The "B" group is all people seeking a change.

The B group includes more people with problems than the A group: all terminated employees, the "personality conflicts," the unemployed, the terminal assignments, the pass-overs, and so on. Mind you, I'm emphatically *not* saying that there are not excellent managers in Group B. You may be an excellent manager and be in Group B. The fact that you have invested in *The Headhunter Strategy* is enough to award you special status. (Sorry, I couldn't resist that.) However, *considered as a group*, there are *more* (greater numbers of) attractive A's than B's.

"Pure" recruiters—Q3's and Q4's—understand this. All "pure" recruiting (or almost all) is restricted to A's. B candidates are considered only when there are *very* good reasons to do so. One of the headhunter's greatest fears is of presenting a candidate with hidden liabilities that are discovered later. Since this jeopardizes *the recruiter's* standing with the client (which is considerably more important to him than *your* standing), recruiters concentrate on A candidates.

Personnel managers also try to concentrate—or *think* they try to concentrate—on hiring A's. That's one of the reasons your resume is scrutinized so closely by the thorough resume reader (remember him?) and employment advertising is so thoroughly screened (more on that in Chapter 7). The personnel manager is "picking" for A candidates.

Hiring managers (the line people who do the hiring, not the personnel people who do the screening) aren't as attuned as headhunters or personnel managers to A versus B status, but will sense it. Has a hiring manager whom you found on your own ever referred you to the personnel manager? When that happened, you were pigeon-holed onto the B track; the hiring manager would have dealt with you personally if you had been perceived as an A.

Make no mistake about this: A's receive stronger consideration than B's. So, regardless of your present status—happy as a clam where you are or you cleaned out your desk last week—if you are going to "look outside" your current organization, be an A in every letter, telephone conversation, and interview.

Remember the A−B principle; you'll see it later in *The Head-hunter Strategy* when we'll help you plan and conduct a self-marketing campaign to reinforce your A status. I want to be very clear about this: *Even if you fall into the B category*—chances are very high you will at least once during your business career and very likely not through any personal fault—*you must appear to the outside world as an* A. A status is the key to strong consideration by headhunters and hiring managers; B's are relegated to "back burner" consideration and are never hired when A's are available. To make your job campaign work most effectively (that is, offer you opportunities for professional and personal growth), you must understand these two categories.

— PART 2 —

THE JOB SEARCH

— 6 —

The Job Search and
The Kitchen Stool

The Headhunter Strategy is definitely *not* intended to be the encyclopedia of jobhunting or changing. Other authors have attacked the general subject repeatedly; there are hundreds of books in print on job changing "systems." This ground has been plowed so often and so deep, we're going to skip the usual "laundry lists" of things to do, how to get organized, and so forth. I'm going to do my best to leave these out and concentrate instead on new—and more effective—ways to approach the problem.

While there are plenty of these books in print, reading more than a handful will subject you to what economists call "diminishing marginal utility." In other words, your twenty-fifth jobhunting book will taste about the same as your twenty-fifth beer.

Time is of the essence in your job campaign; you have neither time to waste with marginally beneficial books nor the luxury of leisure time to reinvent important strategies already invented and in print. These three books—plus the others recommended elsewhere in *THS*— will suffice:

What Color is Your Parachute? A Practical Manual for Job Hunters & Career Changers, Richard N. Bolles, Ten Speed Press, 1984. 377 pages, soft cover, $8.95.

Parachute is updated annually—Bolles relies extensively on feedback from readers. This one is worth reading every year to *reinforce* (not replace) your personal career planning.

One on One: Winning the Hiring Decision, Ted Pettus, Random House, 1979. 189 pages, hard cover, $12.95.

Jobs are won or lost in *interviews*. *One on One* will help you prepare for them and is very useful for the "night before."

Guerrilla Tactics in the Job Market, Tom Jackson, Bantam Books, 1978. 176 pages, $3.50.

Jackson's got some neat tricks. Philosophically, we appear pretty close. He likes personnel people a little better than I do, but doesn't understand headhunters. Example: If you obtain lists of the "best" headhunters from personnel people you know (as Jackson suggests), you're likely to get the weak sister list instead of the ones you want. Still, *GT* is a good book.

Two steps are useful when attacking any complex problem:

1. Identify and isolate the overall problem, then
2. Break the problem into smaller parts for resolution.

There should be scarcely any disagreement that a job campaign at the executive level is a complex task. It's also an important one. What could be more important to you than managing your own destiny? However, that doesn't stop executive after executive from screwing it up. That's unfortunate, because a poorly executed job campaign that leads to the wrong position can cost *years* of your life and leave you undercompensated and underchallenged.

Job campaigning is a project to be attacked with all the vigor and creativity you can muster. The competition you face is as competent as any you have ever faced (or ever will) individually or in the marketplace. There is not much room for luck, either.

You have heard the horror stories about unemployed managers and executives: Out of work for a year (or even longer), marriages breaking up, life savings draining away, and so on. Yet, important jobs go begging. Why?

Digging into psyches is not my forte, but I suspect it has something to do with perceived loss of face that comes with asking for help. Also, following defective advice—and there's plenty of it around—contributes. Want to organize a truly mediocre job campaign? Ask your next door neighbor or brother-in-law for assistance.

Whether you choose to follow the strategies I suggest is strictly up to you. For the most part, the methods I advocate can be used *in addition* to the methods "they" suggest.

Here are the shortcomings common to "average" job campaigns. Measure your plan against these:

Inadequately planned.
Poorly executed.
Important avenues not identified or tested.
Undercapitalized/underbudgeted.

This sounds like the final performance review of the last person

you terminated, doesn't it? Even though you don't tolerate this
sort of performance from yourself or from your subordinates *at the
office*, I have seen enough of your contemporaries fall into the trap
that I must warn you of the dangers.

Two analogies will be helpful:

THE NEW PRODUCT INTRODUCTION
(Your role: Advertising Manager)

Your firm (a consumer products division of a Fortune 500 manu-
facturer) is ready to introduce a major new product to the American public. This product took a number of years to develop,
including heavy R&D, substantial investment in plant, and equipment. The future of this division—and your own career—rests on
the success (or failure) of this new product line.

The advertising budget is limited, so you can't do everything
you would like to do. ("Do they think these things are going to
jump off the shelves into people's pockets?"). However, you do
have complete authority over how ad dollars will be spent.

Now, compare your job campaign to the ad manager's project:

☐   Your investment in yourself—education, years of experience, and "tuition" paid by being "patient" in a position longer
than you should have—is every bit as important as that Fortune
500 firm's investment in plant, equipment, and R&D.

☐   When conducting a job campaign, you have even greater
control of your future than does the ad manager, even if the ad
manager's program is wildly successful. You'll directly reap the
benefits or losses. Success or failure will be shared by all partici-
pants. Even bystanders will take credit for successes.

☐   Unless you have *very* deep pockets, you'll need to make important choices on how to spend the funds available for the job search. The decisions facing you are similar to those facing the ad manager: What combination of promotion vehicles and marketing channels available do you select to yield the greatest possible return?

You are the expert—no one will be looking over your shoulder. And you will bear complete responsibility for the success or failure of the project.

Important point: There are plenty of available positions either vacant or ready to be created meeting all your criteria. But, each one is buried under a separate haystack. The key to turning up the needles—the interesting opportunities representing financial and responsibility upgrades—is using *truck-mounted electromagnets* instead of pitchforks. So, let's organize your job campaign so it will perform as effectively as any project you would tackle at the office.

THE KITCHEN STOOL

Any job search is like a "kitchen stool"—it has several "legs" (these are the promotion vehicles facing the advertising manager). The more "legs" the stool has, the steadier the footing. Three legs are the minimum (unless you are an acrobat) but four legs work best. Most job hunters try to conduct the job campaign on only a leg or two. There's no wonder "average" campaigns produce "average" results.

Here are the "legs" of a complete job campaign, as I see them:

1.   Networking—all the industry, professional, and personal

contacts you can generate plus the "second generation" contacts they produce.

2. Responses to employment advertising.

3. Direct approaches to potential employers you find interesting.

4. Approaches to third parties—the "headhunters."

We have chapters coming up and some nonshopworn wrinkles to suggest for legs 2–4. *The Headhunter Strategy's* primary purpose, though, is to focus on Leg 4, the most neglected part of job hunting: contact with headhunters. I am not discussing networking at all (not because it isn't important; it is) because I have little to add to what others—particularly Bolles, in *Parachute*—have previously written.

Ineffective job searches—as many as 90% of all job campaigns will fit this category—"shortchange" or even exclude one or more of the legs. To maximize your chances for genuine improvement of financial and responsibility levels, you must *use every available noncompeting approach*. Fail to do that and you'll never know what you *didn't* find; you may settle for considerably less than you might have.

So, an effective job campaign isn't one project, it's four projects running concurrently. Let me say that again: *Your job campaign is four projects running concurrently.* Ideally, *each separate approach* will produce one or more solid leads (defined as repeat interviewing), and *more than one offer.* You should also plan each leg of your campaign independently, for best results.

Developing more than one offer is an important goal. I don't consider a "one offer" job campaign successful. Neither should you.

☐   You need two offers—minimum (three or more are even better)—for a sense of your "market value."

☐ "Leave present position/take new position" versus "keep present position/turn down new position" isn't much of a choice. If you are seriously undercompensated/underchallenged where you are, even a *weak* offer may look good. If you are unemployed (or about to be), *any* offer looks good.

Multiple approaches yield multiple offers. Do your best to bring them along at comparable speeds, so that you'll have a real choice to make when the offers come.

To complete this chapter, here are the *general rules of effectiveness* for any job campaign. You should be looking for ways to apply each of these in every component of your search:

1. Look for ways to *cause interviews to happen.*

New positions are won through *interviews*, not networking, not slick resumes, not creative letters, not telephone calls. Don't confuse efforts with results, either. If you're not causing interviews to take place, something is seriously wrong with your job search. Press Rule 1 against your forehead; it's the most important concept in this book.

2. Look for ways to *minimize your competition.*

You'll always do better when potential employers compare you with fewer and weaker candidates. One of the most important ways to do that is by maximizing your contacts with top-level decisionmakers who have placed "screens" in front of them to discourage contacts. Locating and approaching top-level managers isn't that difficult; I'll show you how in Chapter 8.

3. Look for ways to *lever your efforts.*

Remember the new product intro? You must obtain maximum

"reach" from the money, time, and effort you have available to spend on the project.

4. Look for ways to *make yourself look desirable* to potential employers.

You'll be seeing these four rules again and again in the rest of *THS*. Now, let's get started on legs 2, 3, and 4.

— 7 —

Employment Advertising

The employment advertising routine is one of the most diabolical inventions of modern man, particularly at executive levels. Do you relish having your executive-level credentials and life's accomplishments measured by clerks and secretaries? That is exactly what will happen to many of your answers to advertisements.

More hopes are raised—and dashed—through employment advertising than by any other means I can think of, unless you consider lottery ticket sales in the ghetto. Even there, the odds may be better.

I'm inclined to advise you not to bother suffering through the humiliation of answering employment advertising, but you would listen politely—then do it anyway. So, I won't do that. Employment advertising *is* important to the job hunter, but mostly when used another way. Some background and analysis first:

Four major U.S. dailies account for *almost all*—90% or better—of executive-level employment advertising in the United States—only four. They are: Sunday editions of *The New York*

Times, The Chicago Tribune, and *The Los Angeles Times,* plus Tuesday editions (with minor spill-over into Wednesdays) of the four regional editions of *The Wall Street Journal.* (Read Dow Jones' *National Business Employment Weekly* for last week's advertising from the four regional *WSJ* editions.)

The correlation between location of vacancies advertised and a given paper is fairly high, but not absolute. Because corporations are not wild about assuming relocation expenses of new hires, they'll advertise close to home and skip remote exposure. Regional advertising is also cheaper than advertising in the four major nationally read newspapers.

If you have a definitive relocation goal, take a short-term subscription to the major newspaper in that city as a companion, but don't be surprised if the most interesting ads are duplicated in *WSJ* or elsewhere.

All these newspapers can be found at major newsstands, the airport, or major libraries, but a 3- or 6-month mail subscription is more practical. (Libraries frown on your marking up and cutting up their newspapers, for example.) Each welcomes short-term subscriptions for its Sunday edition. (After all, they are in the business of selling newspapers.) To save shoe leather and telephone time, here is contact information for the top four, and subscription rates (Sundays only; information was current when *THS* went to press):

The New York Times
Mail Subscription Dept.
P.O. Box 5792
New York, NY 10087
1–800–631–2500
3 months $43.03
6 months $77.38
1 year $140.20

The Chicago Tribune
435 North Michigan Avenue
Chicago, IL 60611
312–222–4100
3 months $25.50
6 months $48.50
1 year $86.00

The Los Angeles Times
Circulation Department
Times Mirror Square
Los Angeles, CA 90053
1–800–528–4637
8 weeks $16.00
16 weeks $32.00
24 weeks $48.00

The National Business Employment Weekly (*NBEW*) combines employment advertising from the four regional editions of *WSJ*.

NBEW
Box 9100
Springfield, MA 01101
1–800–453–4100
8 weeks $32.00

Send a check with your order; these folks want money up front. *NBEW* will accept MC, Visa, AMEX and Diner's credit cards for mail-order subscriptions; send complete account number, expiration date, and sign your order. (Only *The New York Times* will bill you for your subscription.)

Employment advertising doesn't work very well, but not for the reasons you think. It certainly is expensive. To run an attractive 4-inch by 2-column ad (average size) in *The Wall Street Journal*'s "National Edition" *one time* would cost $4,216.80, excluding typeset, paste-up, and copywriting. But, replies come from the wrong people—overwhelmingly. They fall into three distinct categories:

☐   B's. (See Chapter 6.)

☐   Those not remotely qualified. Incredibly, some job seekers will routinely answer *every ad in the newspaper*. I have seen books and "systems" recommending this method.

> Responding to your recent advertisement for Vice President of Manu-facturing—Nuclear Submarines, I am interested in associating with your fine organization. I am currently a regional sales manager for a major encyclopedia publisher. While I haven't previously sold submarines, I am certain I could, and am looking for a new challenge. Let's schedule an interview at a convenient time to discuss my qualifications and potential contributions to your firm.

While I am not particularly interested in sharpshooting some-one else's "system," if you are using this method, consider another equally effective: the unique one-way resume sending system in your bathroom. Results are about the same, and you'll save con-siderable postage expense. While it might be fun to speculate about an attractive job at the firm advertising for something out of your area of expertise, there is a much better way to approach that firm. We'll get to it.

☐   Headhunters scratching for business. Many headhunters use employment advertising as a prospecting tool. Their chances are a little better than yours, but still poor.

The company running the advertising hopes that at least a *few* candidates judged to be A's will respond. But even if you are an A—or a "nonproblem B" your chances are still poor at best.

An employment manager (Fortune 500 Corp.) I know recently told me his last national *Wall Street Journal* ad produced *two bushels* of letters and resumes. I finally got the assignment—and filled it—after the company tired of reviewing B backgrounds. Headhunters are paid to deliver A candidates, remember? A's didn't read the want ads.

Who do you think is going to sift through those piles of resumes? Your potential boss? Guess again— the line manager has too many more important and immediate things to do (like handling personal responsibilities as well as those of the empty job). The logging in, shuffling, and screening will be delegated to a paper-shuffler/screener with decisions made on a scoring basis, off a "wish list" of qualifications, or even whimsically. This person is usually a low-level personnel functionary; the *head* personnel functionary is busy with *really* important things, like crafting the new (improved) salary administration procedure. If you are *very* fortunate, the hiring manager's *secretary* will handle the job. How does it feel to have an $18,000 per year personnel clerk or the bosses' secretary evaluating your potential contribution to the firm? Yes, the clerk or secretary will most likely be the "designated resume reader"—even for positions at substantial salary levels, *if the position was advertised nationally.*

Let's digress for just a minute on two important side issues:

☐ As expensive as major newspaper advertising is and in spite of the additional expense it generates for the firm (resumes to shuffle, telephone calls to make, wasted interviewing trips, etc.) *it's still less expensive for the firm than using third-parties, but only if it works.* Engaging a headhunter to fill a $60,000 position will cost the firm $18,000 in fees (30% of annual salary is the "going rate"), plus the headhunter's candidates still have to be interviewed and other expenses paid. You can do a lot of papershuffling for the $13,000+ difference, so many firms will "chase rainbows" through employment advertising. Another favorite story in the search business is the one about the "legendary" Harvard MBA with 10 years experience who will work for $20,000 per year. The headhunters can't find him, neither will newspaper advertising.

☐   Personnel people will scream "foul" at much of this chapter (and the rest of the book, no doubt). Some of that attitude stems from the "dog and cat" relationship between headhunters and personnel people; I'll admit that my perspective is 100% headhunter, and therefore, skewed. *However*, the personnel department is corporate bureaucracy. Bureaucrats are drawn to ponderous departments where they can practice their bureaucratic skills; line managers aren't bureaucrats (if they were, they'd be personnel managers). Headhunters exist, in part, because personnel people aren't good at recruiting; line managers are too busy tending the store. If personnel had its way, everyone would read their want ads (except their own people, of course). But B's read ads more than A's and the headhunters won't go away. Here's a suggestion for any personnel manager who feels his ox has been unfairly gored: Write a book about managing careers through personnel managers.

So, employment advertising doesn't work very well because:

You are tossed in with a huge pile of the wrong people.
The wrong people do the screening and shuffling.

Someone else wrote the rules of the game and these rules are completely unfavorable to anyone answering the advertising.

Thus far in this chapter, we have dealt only with "open" advertising, which clearly identifies the firm with the vacancy (or sometimes, the headhunter with the assignment). There is another kind—the "blind" ad—where no firm is identified. Blind ads represent the ultimate head trip for sadists who enjoy the attentions of masochistic candidates. No telling who you'll turn up in one of these nets.

"Our employees are aware of this ad." The check is in the mail. I'll respect you in the morning. If you are gainfully employed and would be embarrassed if your present boss found out you were "looking," answering this ad would be insane. (All major papers—including *WSJ*—*allegedly* will prevent your applying for your own job this way: When you address your letter to Box E162, *Wall Street Journal*, etc., put your resume and cover letter inside *another blank envelope*. On the inside blank envelope, write: "Note: To be sent to any company except . . ." The newspaper's clerks will theoretically protect you by *not* sending your letter to the company you specify if that company is the "blind" advertiser. My senses tell me this is a *very* thin lifeline.)

A better strategy might be to answer the ad through a friend, camouflaging your identity and present employer. Keep in mind, though, that because a bureaucrat wrote the ad and will manage the firm's response, your conservatism will most likely be interpreted as failure to follow instructions. This is a screen-out offense in bureaucratic eyes that will probably eliminate you from consideration. Too many other candidates will follow the instructions; unusual responses don't fit well into scoring systems.

Here's another little trick that might work: Pick a cooperative business school professor, attorney, CPA, or other professional friend. Ask them to write a letter answering the ad, saying something like this.

Gentlemen:

I noticed your recent *WSJ* advertisement for VP-Manufacturing while checking my bond portfolio. It occurred to me that John Jones (my former student, or client, or whatever), who is well known to me, is uniquely qualified for the position. You might want to check his interest in the position. Contact him at 212–555–1234.

Sincerely,

James T. Smith
Professor of Business

"Resumes without salary history will not be considered." It's not clear that resumes *with* salary history will be considered either. You'll see this on open and blind advertising. This ploy is one of the favorites of personnel departments conducting compensation surveys.

Example:

A Fortune 500 firm is facing a mutiny in its marketing ranks. Headhunters have been picking off the best of the product managers. Exit interviews indicate the firm is undercompensating the marketing staff and they are bailing out for more money at other firms. Fortune 500 has tried to uncover the competitive rate for marketing people, but competitors won't tell (or worse, they are giving salaries, but lying about it; this is a major problem with straightforward and "above board" compensation surveys).

So for $5,000 or so—the price of the advertising is less expensive than one of the major human resource consulting firms will charge, anyway—a Fortune 500 firm can assemble a nice blind ad for "Vice President—Marketing" that will flush out plenty of letters from promotable group product managers. "Resumes without salary history will not be considered." The firm will receive lots of data on the earnings of product managers, then use the data to adjust marketing compensation levels.

This sort of trick is also practiced by headhunters. Remember, your clues to the identity of the blind advertiser are limited or worse. Note also that the papers *do not* require that major corporate advertisers actually have a position to fill; this is one of those questions that is never asked. Nor is there any followup on the part of the newspaper, except by a sales rep to ask for more advertising.

This is one of the areas where state regulators have "cleaned up" the "agency" business: There was a time when agencies would advertise the "Executive Assistant to Television Producer" vacancy or some such. When the bright-eyed candidate showed up to interview for this glamorous position, she found that it had "just" been filled; how about the clerk-typist's position at Acme Storm Door, instead? Bait and switch is a strict no-no and has just about been wrung out of headhunter advertising today. The practice is "abusive and unethical" for agencies, but all in a day's work for many major firms and out of reach of the state regulators.

"Blind" ads border on being evil; there are too many ways they can be abused. "Open" ads are expensive and ineffective. Skip both; there is a better way to use the advertising.

TURNING THE TABLES ON EMPLOYMENT ADVERTISING

Here are two "non-shopworn" strategies to try. Each has the potential for beating the pants off the "standard reply" to the help-wanted ad. Also, if they feel too heretical for you, each can be used *in addition* to your "standard replies" without hurting your chances.

Strategy 1

Consider the interesting ad to be one thing only: A solid lead that a position of interest *may* be available. Disregard all ad instructions; we're going to short-circuit the system. The advertising program is almost certainly being orchestrated by the personnel department. The human resources people are going to be busy with the paperwork for a while, shuffling, scoring, and classifying their resumes. You have a temporary *window of opportunity* to track down the appropriate line manager, and make your own contact.

It's very important to keep and protect your A status, so do not mention the ad at all. Refer to the ad, and you risk being shuffled onto the side track with personnel department candidates, and B status. A bit of corporate psychology here will also encourage you.

Personnel departments are *not* held in high esteem by line managers in most organizations. Personnel work is generally regarded as a housekeeping detail, on a par with ordering pencils and turning out lights. Final selection of candidates for line positions is rarely done by the personnel department, even when line management delegates recruiting. Rather, personnel will laboriously winnow down the applicants to a handful of semi-finalists. These will be referred to the line manager for another cut or two, before an offer is made.

Even "high-flying" titles—Director of Personnel, Vice President-Human Resources, etc.—are no guarantee this particular manager carries an important stick in the organization. Texans have a saying worth remembering: "All hat, no cattle." So look for the line manager with troops, not necessarily the high-flying title.

My skepticism of personnel departments relates primarily to recruiting efforts and management of individual careers. Remember, if personnel people were as proficient as they claim to be, there would be no headhunters. Even those major firms with staff "recruiters" use third-party recruiters; the "corporate recruiter" may be responsible for directing the third-party efforts. But most staff "recruiters" just advertise and screen for line management.

By making a direct contact with the correct line manager, you'll leapfrog over the long line of people playing games with the personnel department. With a good impression, you'll be considered at least as favorably as any of the personnel department referrals —they are all B's, remember? Protect your A status and *do not* mention that ad. After personnel has screened all of those respondents, you may have completed several interviews—and be getting close to an offer. Because the line manager "found" you himself (herself), his (her) vested interest in you will give you an important edge over personnel department candidates.

Forget trying to track down the blind ad unless you have a brother-in-law at the newspaper to do your legwork. Far too often, they are run for reasons other than filling jobs. I know a national sales manager who enjoyed running blind ads just so he could tweak his chief competitor's nose by pointing out that the competitor's salesmen were unhappy. You might also learn that it's *your* company advertising to fill *your* job.

Strategy 2

In the first part of this chapter, we established that employment advertising is overwhelmingly stacked in the favor of the advertiser, particularly when running "blind" ads. With the "blind" ad, the advertiser camouflages the identity of the firm and prevents informing competitors of a sensitive vacancy. Antsy, but unpromotable (or about to be terminated) current employees don't find out about the vacancy until too late to do anything about it. Replies can be thoroughly screened—at the advertiser's convenience.

So, run your *own* blind ad. You'll benefit from the same advantages enjoyed by the major advertisers.

> *The Wall Street Journal* will forward all replies to you at home and unopened (the "blind box" service costs $11.92 extra).

Camouflage your identity; bosses, peers, and subordinates won't be aware of your availability. Your present position won't be jeopardized.

> Review replies at your convenience, then act on the ones that sound interesting.

Each Tuesday and Wednesday (employment advertising days, remember?), *WSJ* includes a "Positions Wanted" section. Count the ads in this section; you'll rarely see more than a dozen—six or eight is about average. One franchised recruiting organization —Robert Half (EDP/finance/accounting specialists)—usually accounts for about half (no pun intended) of these. Because Half offices are regular advertisers, the system is also effective for candidate marketing (Q2); you can be sure they wouldn't be throwing money away repeating ads that do not work.

That same $527.10 per column inch will also apply to you, but 1 inch (or less) is plenty—You can squeeze quite a bit of abbreviated copy into the space. You can also cut the cost considerably by using a regional edition. For example, if you want to focus on Dallas, don't say Dallas, just run it in the Southwest edition (that $527.10 "National Edition" column inch costs $66.08 in the Southwest edition) or wherever else, at similar savings. (Midwest: $166.88; Eastern: $215.32; Western: $118.02; all prices in effect when *THS* went to press.)

WSJ circulation is massive—over 2 million per day with considerable "pass-along" readership. The same reason this paper is an attractive advertising vehicle for employers commends it to you: Your ad will be read a *lot* of times.

To determine how a "Position Wanted" ad would pull replies, I tried one myself, composing an ad for a midlevel marketing manager looking to associate with a smaller firm. Results? *54 replies*, including several interesting nibbles from CEO's—one from the owner of a Lake Tahoe casino looking for a marketing manager (that was a neat one)—an assortment of "get-rich-quick" and "pyramiding" schemes (Amways, Shaklees, a "miracle" gas stretcher for *any* carburetor, etc.)—be prepared for a few annoying replies to your PW ad and for some with a high nuisance value (they'll be irrelevant when you use a blind box)—and many letters from headhunters with assignments for marketing managers. And—incredibly—I also received several resumes from jobhunters (I told you some people answer *all WSJ* ads!).

Writing abbreviated copy for "Position Wanted" ads is a little tricky. You have only enough space to include one large hook or a couple of little ones. Review a few of these (Tuesday/Wednesday *WSJ*'s and the samples at the end of this chapter) to get the flavor of how they are done. As you examine them, you'll quickly see which are effective and which are not. My advice on these: don't try to accomplish too much. Start with fifty words or so, and go to work on your ad with a red pencil, taking it down to the skeleton. Then, show it to someone else to insure the copy is clear and understandable. "Non-directed" ads—those that present no clear picture of what you want to do or what you are qualified to do—are unlikely to produce valuable response.

Act on this quickly, though. If *WSJ* becomes filled with these ads, the effectiveness will be diluted. Wednesday (the lighter of the employment advertising days) may be better than Tuesday, where PW's can get lost or buried in display advertising purchased by major firms. Review the copywriting section of Chapter 10 for some additional thoughts.

You could try the same project in your industry or functional-specific trade publications. Because the trade magazines focus narrowly on a specific industry or functional area, readership is well targeted. Trade magazine advertising is generally inexpensive, but because circulation is limited to a narrow field, you'll cut down the universe of opportunities substantially. Even so, an inexpensive position-wanted ad in your major industry publication might be worth a try.

Position-wanted advertising in newspapers other than *The Wall Street Journal* tends to be buried at the end of the general help wanted section. Major metropolitan newspaper PW sections are usually dominated by butchers, bakers, and candlestick makers. They probably are not worth the expense, so skip them.

Here's another to *definitely* skip: Several times a year, *The National Business Employment Weekly* (NBEW), Dow Jones' weekly newspaper of *WSJ* employment advertising, runs a special "Talent for Hire" section. Ads are cheap and they fill a number of pages each time the section runs. But circulation is minor (about 75,000 per week) compared to *WSJ*. Individual ads are buried in the pile; I've been unable to observe any sort of order by function, salary desired, or organizational level. Also, who's going to read them? Other jobseekers? (Jobseekers are NBEW's primary audience.) Forget it.

SAMPLE POSITION WANTED ADS

POSITIONS WANTED

CHIEF FINANCIAL OFFICER
Energetic aggressive results-oriented shirt sleeve executive offers over fifteen years of significant experience & an outstanding & extensive record in operational-oriented financial functions, analysis, cost control & M.I.S. Exceptionally skilled in profit improvement, inventory control, E.D.P. design & implementation & cash flow management. Highly regarded in the business, professional & banking community. Excellent communicator & people motivator. (201) 944‑   or Box ES-   , Wall Street Journal

WHAT CAN I DO FOR YOU?
Farmer, Export Mgr. Founded Foreign Subsidiary. Well Traveled. Trilingual. Wide Experience. Have papers to reside in Mexico, 65 years and good health.   1501
, Tx

BANK CONTROLLER – CPA/ MBA. Recognized pro in this sector. Implements new budgeting for depts, respon for tax planning, merger valuations, prod costing & the overall supvsn of the bank's acctg posture. Amenable to reloc. $41K
ROBT HALF of NY, Inc/agency 522 5 Av NYC 10036   212-221-6500

WELL TESTING SPECIALIST
OIL & GAS. Age 33, Mech. Eng. bkgd. Hardworking, reliable with sense of responsibility. Presently working in Middle East. Seeking position in USA or abroad.
Box ES-   , Wall Street Journal

POSITIONS WANTED

Corporate Finance/Syndicate Financ. prin of broker dealer firm, wishes to relocate to London or Geneva-Lausanne area. 10 yrs exp & extensive industry contacts. Reply
Box ES-   Wall Street Journal

Young 60 year old executive seeks full P&L responsibility with heavy metal fabricating company in Phila. area. Compensation package in low 6 figures required. Reply to
Box ES-   , Wall Street Journal

EUROPEAN SALES/MKTG REP – Engineer Belgium resident, also familiar Africa, Middle-East. Exp pumps, filters & fluid controls. Former sales & gen'l mngr of U.S. firm.
212-944-

PURCHASE MANAGER Hdq – Plant experience. Expertise energy, chemicals. Desire metro NY/NE challenge. BS Chem 1969, MBA 1972. Quiet leader
Box ES-   , Wall Street Journal

MBA seeks career opportunity in NYC. Growth oriented people person looking to make the right connection. Let's explore the possibilities.
718-275-

N.Y.S.E. Branch Office Mgr. R.O.P. 10 years discount exp. seeks to open or manage branch office in Northern New England.
Box ES-   , Wall Street Journal

Experienced Trainer, PhD student, seeks P/T positions consulting, teaching. Computer literacy specialist.
Box ES   Wall Street Journal

The sample "Position Wanted" ads shown were lifted from a recent Tuesday copy of *WSJ*'s Eastern Edition. (I've blocked out Box #'s, telephones, and addresses so we won't embarrass anyone.) This group of ads is reasonably representative of what you'll see. The worst ad is probably the first one. This CFO could have said more in half the space. Words like "Energetic aggresive results-oriented shirt sleeve executive" smack of B status, don't they? (You're getting the hang of this.) Long laundry lists of "expertise" won't be read or believed. Contrast this with the Robert Half ad: It accomplishes more with less copy. Keep your PW ad simple and avoid overkill.

"MBA" looks as though he/she meant to mail the ad to a singles magazine instead of *WSJ*. Results of non-directed ads like this one are very predictable.

Put a little snap into the copy; it may be helpful to visualize yourself as a copywriter when composing your ad. "Farmer" did, even if the ad was non-directed. "Experienced Trainer" could have said something like "I'll teach your smart people to talk to dumb computers."

If you decide to invest limited job campaigning dollars in a *WSJ* PW ad, have someone critique your efforts before submitting it. These are *expensive* bullets too valuable to waste.

= 8 =

Approaching
Potential Employers

Locating, evaluating, and approaching firms that can potentially use your services is one of four "legs" of your job search. On a four-legged stool, is leg 2 more important than leg 3? Obviously not; each of four legs is equally important.

Curiously, this leg is neglected; it's often one of those half-finished projects mentioned earlier in the book—too many job-seekers concentrate on employment advertising at the expense of a little basic research. That's a shame, because direct approaches yield the "most" new positions.

How many is "most"? The answer would be a guess, not a statistic. Anyone waving a number around here would have to perform some awfully expensive research and canvassing. They would have to:

1. Calculate the total number of positions created, then filled.

2. Add the total number of positions vacated, then filled.

3. Subtract the number of positions advertised and filled by advertising from the sum of 1 and 2.

4. Subtract the number advertised but filled by third parties.

5. Subtract the number never advertised that were filled by third parties.

6. Subtract the number filled by employer direct approaches to known candidates.

Because there are so many unknowns in the equation, anyone waving around "authoritative" numbers more likely is blowing smoke. Even full-time government statisticians waffle and revise estimates on numbers of people working or unemployed at a given time. The strongest statement I'm going to make is that more positions are filled through direct approaches than through other means—and that's a seat-of-the-pants guess.

Direct approaches yield the most new positions because they are the most efficient (read this as less expensive) for the employer. It doesn't cost the employer extra to receive letters or telephone calls, candidates assume all costs.

Why contact employers directly? For the simple reason that positions are vacated daily by promotions, demotions, resignations, terminations, retirements, deaths, and so on. Positions are also created every day.

Some portion of vacant and created positions will reach headhunters and/or employment advertising; most "experts" claim more than half never will. So without debating percentages, the direct approach is an important "market" you should not neglect.

There is another important reason for direct approaches: Reach the proper line manager with a persuasive story; the position you want may be created for you. If you can persuade a decisionmaker you will produce more (or produce greater savings) than you will cost, *you will be hired*. This concept is critical; you must drive this message home in all interviews and in all copy you write.

Locating potential employers is a project that cannot be "winged" and still be effective. There is no way you can know who they might be without some basic research even if you are an expert in your functional area or industry. Relying on *recollections* of industry players is inefficient, undependable, and incomplete.

You now have two research assignments—one mandatory, the other optional.

LIBRARY REFERENCE SECTION RESEARCH

This is a minor project. About 8 hours of research in the reference section of an average-sized library will do the job. This assignment doesn't even have to be done by you. Hire a bright high school senior or college student to do it for you if you like. It's an easy project, but necessary.

Step 1. Determine the industries of interest to you and those industries where you have some particular expertise. Make a list; be generous at this stage—include all of them—you're going to cut down the list later.

Step 2. Off to the library's reference section for your basic research in three books (I told you this was easy).

(a) Ask the librarian for help in locating the Standard Industrial Classification (SIC) book. There are several versions;

the one you choose makes no difference. The Department of Labor publishes one, as does the Office of Management and Budget (OMB) and there are commercial ones. Look up the SIC's of your areas of interest and add a few more; the SIC book will give you other ideas. Be sure to include SIC's *close* to your areas of expertise. This will help increase your prospect list to be developed next.

(b) Armed with SIC's of interest, go to *Dun's Million Dollar Directory* (there are three volumes), which (thoughtfully) lists all U.S. firms (of a million plus in sales or assets; I don't remember which, but it doesn't matter) listed by SIC. Make another list of firms interesting to you (eliminate those too small, too big, the ones you know but aren't interested in, parts of the country too hot, too cold, etc.). If you were not able to find an SIC book, there is a condensed version of the SIC list in *Dun's*. There's only one more book to look at (two, if you're really dedicated).

(c) Last stop: *Standard & Poor's Register*. Volume 1 (Corporations) lists the officers (with areas of responsibility) of the corporations from your *Dun's* list and complete corporate addresses. Continue your list. Now to Volume 2 (Directors and Executives). Look up each officer by name. About half are listed *with home addresses*. Notice that each listing includes a short biography of the executive including age, schools attended, and so on. You'll certainly want to come back to Volume 2 during interview preparation; you'll want to weave some of this information into the interview to demonstrate your advance preparation.

Step 3. Plan your direct mail campaign and prepare your letter (use copywriting tips in Chapter 10).

Total out-of-pocket expense of this research is $0; $50 if you hired an assistant. An outplacement firm will include this as part of its program and will sell it to you for several thousand dollars (or more), but the information provided will steer you to whom they think you should contact. Your list will be very different: higher quality and more extensive. (I told you this book was worth its price.) *You* pick the ones you want to approach, not someone else.

Nose around a bit more while you are in the reference section. The Dun & Bradstreet *Reference Book of Corporate Management* is competitive with Standard & Poor's *Register*, but doesn't have bios of officers or home addresses. The library may also have state manufacturers directories (published by a variety of private firms, state departments of commerce, and so forth) that are worth a look. Take note of *Moody's* and *Value Line* books; they discuss the financial performance, basic businesses, and general state of all public companies. You'll want to come back to these for interview preparation.

Larger reference sections may have other directories and source materials not listed.

COMMERCIAL EXECUTIVE LISTS

This is the "optional" research project. It carries a significant, but affordable, cost. My fellow headhunters may want to drum me out of the business after I reveal one of their most important and effective "tricks," but here goes.

Every industry and functional specialty has trade publications. Every one. You already know what they are if you are a well-read executive, and you probably have a pile of back issues quietly gathering dust somewhere. One of these is usually recognized as the "lighthouse" of the industry or functional area—and is faithfully read by *every* important executive. Most trade publications "mine" their subscription lists extensively by renting the names, titles, and addresses of subscribers to other firms. The buyers of the data then use the lists to offer their products and services to a well-targeted audience: Welcome to the computer age and direct mail selling.

You are probably familiar with the explosive growth of *direct marketing* in the United States. Through the computerized approach, marketers can approach tiny and undisturbed markets for goods and services. The key factors are:

☐ Market Segmentation and Targeting. Only prime buyers are approached.

☐ Predictability. Favorable responses are small, but consistent.

☐ Economy. Cost per sale is typically a small percentage of the sales price and avoids heavy fixed costs associated with other marketing channels.

☐ Ease of Entry. All it takes to sell by direct mail is the proper prospect list, effective copy, a good product, and a competitive price.

Now we're going to apply the direct marketing approach to your job campaign.

Trade publications are produced by either commercial publishers or trade organizations. Both will rent their lists although commercial publishers are generally less restrictive about it. Remember the card you fill out each year that "qualifies" you for the subscription? You list the number of employees you supervise, major products produced by your firm, size of the firm, your title, and so forth. All of this information is patiently and efficiently sorted by the computer and accessible by any commercial buyer of the data—and you. Make a list of "computer sorts" that would be useful for your job campaign: title of your potential boss, size of the firm, products, location (by zip codes), and so on. Here is the other info you'll need to determine before purchasing your list: price per thousand names, "upcharges" per thousand on the additional "sorts" you want, availability of home addresses, and the minimum order quantity.

Call (or write) the magazine and ask for the person who manages the mailing list. Don't be apologetic or timid about the contact; you're a paying customer about to rent a portion of their mailing list. Obtain the answers to all your questions—they'll probably have a demographic profile of their data they'll send you—then order your list. Your order should be in writing with a check; they'll most likely want payment in advance for a one-time order.

A typical order would look something like this (fictitious entries):

Basic List Price:	$40/M
Upcharge for titles:	5/M
Upcharge for zip codes:	5/M
Upcharge for home addresses:	5/M
Upcharge for products manufactured:	5/M
TOTAL COST	$60/M

"Pressure-sensitive" labels will be available—they "peel and stick"—but I discourage using them, even though it's easier. They are more expensive: $8–10 extra per thousand, and you will be pitching a lot of them. It's also easy for your prospects to identify a piece of computer-generated mail; this works against you, because it detracts from the impact. Pressure-sensitive labels have the mass produced look you'll be working hard to avoid. They work just fine for sales brochures produced by most of the people purchasing the data, but are ineffective for job campaigns. Instead, order the "four-up cheshire" format. There is nothing complicated about this; you just have to understand the lingo. "Four-up" means you'll get four columns of names, titles, and addresses. "Cheshire" refers to the machine that cuts up the printout (regular 11 inch x 15 inch computer paper) into label-size bites and applies it to envelopes.

After you receive your printout (a normal "turnaround" for the publication to get the data to you is 10 days), review it carefully for the executives you decide to approach; circle those with a red felt-tip for entry at the secretarial service. If you planned your list order well, picked several SIC's, and weren't overly restrictive in selecting your mailing prospects, you should have developed a "hot list" of 300–500 key managers. Don't attempt many more than this. That would be overkill as well as being prohibitively expensive to type and mail.

Total out-of-pocket costs = $300, based on a minimum order of 5000 names (typical minimum order quantity, but you may be able to talk them into less) at $40 per thousand, plus $20 per thousand worth of "a la carte" extra computer sorts. This is a high-side estimate; you may be able to get your list for as little as $100.

For either direct mail approach, home addresses are best:

No secretary or other insulation at home to screen the mail.

Mail is read every day rather than being set aside.

Impact is greater.

"Office insulation" is an important issue. Many key executives *never get to see mail addressed to them* —someone intercepts it first. Headhunters call the interceptors "corporate gatekeepers." We'll give you some ideas on sidestepping gatekeepers in the next chapter.

For total out-of-pocket costs of $350 ($50 for your library assistant and $300 for your custom mailing list; this is the high-side estimate), you have produced a mailing list containing the majority of the executives in your industries of interest. Your list includes officers and all your potential bosses, many with home addresses to maximize the impact of your mailing program.

As for telephone approaches, personal visits, smoke signals, or similar means to make contact, read other books on job campaign strategy. I think these means of contact are too expensive, time-consuming, unpredictable, and unproductive.

— 9 —

Approaching Headhunters

As we discussed in Chapter 2, now you know there are four distinct categories of "headhunters." You may have guessed (correctly) that there is a distinct strategy for approaching each class. Skip the Q1's. If you write to them, they'll fill your mailbox with slick proposals of how you have been "selected" for their "executive marketing" programs. (If you choose to have yourself "marketed" by a Q1—particularly the "individual" as opposed to the "corporate" Q1—you are on your own.)

I am generally negative about Q1's, which may be unfortunate, because there may be some good work being performed by Q1's. *May* be; I haven't seen any, but I haven't gone out of my way to look, either. So, I'll label this section as opinion.

Here are the problems I have noticed with Q1's:

☐ The programs are personnel department-oriented. That's not surprising, because many corporate personnel people ultimately drift into outplacement work. By now, you know what I think of personnel-oriented job campaigns; line management-oriented campaigns are more effective.

☐ The programs are overpriced. If offered outplacement assistance from your company, take the cash equivalent if you have a choice. Research and orchestrate your own word-processed correspondence campaign. Any secretarial service with a Wang, Lanier, IBM, or other state-of-the-art machine can handle the word processing component easily. You can handle the potential employer research in one day. (See Chapter 8.)

☐ Repetitive outplacement programs produced by the same firm bear a cookie-cutter resemblance to each other, which definitely *works against* you. On the very day this was written, I received two packages of materials (two different candidates) obviously produced by the same Q1. Even when examined independently, it was apparent the materials were ghost-written. Believe me, headhunters recognize ghostwritten materials. They are just a little too "slick."

☐ "Would you buy a used car from this man?" The Q1 end of the business has been given *two* black eyes by greedy promoters whose selling-to-the-prospect abilities were considerably stronger than their outplacement programs. I'm not going to name names here, but before you fork over a couple of mortgage payments, ask for references—and check them. Have your attorney look over the contract before signing. Performance guarantees typically are absent, your advances aren't refundable, and Q1's leave themselves plenty of loopholes to blame any failure of the program on *you*, not them.

☐ Two of the "biggies"—Jameson and Haldane—have commercially published books outlining their "systems." They are *The Professional Job Changing System* (the Jameson book) and

Bernard Haldane Associates' Job & Career Building. Plow through one of these before deciding on outplacement assistance, but even the books are overpriced; *Parachute* is better, and it's cheap (1984 edition, $8.95).

☐   There is a basic problem with "hand-holding" programs: a "Catch 22." If you are a competent, rational manager, you should be capable of producing an effective self-marketing program. If you are not a competent, rational manager, no outplacement program will turn you into one. Maybe outplacement will help if you are lazy and have deep pockets. Up to you.

Q2's, Q3's, and Q4's fill vacancies for their corporate clients by different means. Therefore, they should be approached differently. (We'll continue to refer to each category of firm by its Recruiting Model© quadrant, so review Chapter 3 if necessary.)

If a quick job change is imperative, realize that you're in the 2-minute drill, down a touchdown *and* a field goal. The game's not over, but you need a quick score, to cover the onside kick, then score again. Strategies, discussed in Chapters 8, 9, and 10, are like the series of plays for the 2-minute drill. They are effective, but high risk. Next time, have a regular game plan (covered in Chapters 13, 14, and 15).

Of all the headhunters in the world, which ones do you approach? Ideally, that is, if cost (considered in dollars and time) were not a constraint, you would want *every* known third party to the hiring process to be aware of your credentials. Some recruiter somewhere has a position perfect for you. But, I have identified *over 20,000* firms in the business. Approaching all of them would exceed the time and financial resources of most job seekers. Also, because the Seattle recruiter specializing in aerospace engineers likely has little use for Miami financial managers, the *cost-effective* solution is to approach recruiters specializing in your *industry* and *functional areas* of expertise. Be certain to approach *both* groups. Headhunters tend to concentrate their recruiting either functionally or on an industry basis.

☐   *Functional* specialists trade on specific functional expertise: finance, engineering, sales, and so forth. These recruiters often have personal experience in their specialty: A former product manager may specialize in marketing assignments. Functional specialists will recruit in that area for a number of clients often in a number of industries. Most functional areas support large numbers of recruiters. Functional specialists typically have more clients than industry specialists, because it takes more clients to keep a functional portfolio full than an industry portfolio. If your functional credentials are more important than your industry credentials, concentrate on this group of recruiters.

☐   *Industry* specialists develop expertise in a particular industry, or industry group, and seek a variety of functional assignments within that industry: The oil/gas/energy industry specialist might recruit operations engineers, geologists, landmen, financial analysts and so forth, all with energy industry expertise. Like the functional specialist, the industry specialist often has personal industry experience. Because he or she depends on multiple assignments from single clients, the industry specialist tends to have a smaller circle of clients than the functional specialist. Any well-defined industry will support a large number of recruiters. If your industry credentials are more important than your functional credentials, concentrate on this group of recruiters.

So, to maximize your exposure to the "assignment pool," contact both groups. The financial analyst with a major bank looks for the recruiters specializing in the finance/accounting *function* and in the banking *industry*. The electrical engineering manager with a major food processor mails to engineering specialists and food specialists. And so on. Mail to both groups; "overlap" is minimal.

If your job search includes *specific location goals*—you'll only be happy in Orange County, you must stay in Cleveland to tend your condo investments, the doctor says move to Phoenix, whatever, contact *all known recruiters* (*not* just the specialists in the area) *in addition to* your specialist contacts:

☐ While the correlation between the recruiter's location and his/her assignments *is not* absolute, *it is high*. The Miami recruiter will have more Miami assignments than the Los Angeles recruiter.

☐ A legitimate desire to move to, or remain in, a given area, is one factor recruiters (and employers) *will* consider, even if it isn't a major one.

☐ Even "specialists" accept assignments and consider credentials of candidates outside specific areas of interest when there are important reasons to do so—a regular client requests it; the recruiter is aware of a vacancy, but isn't acting on it because of unfamiliarity with the functional area, etc.

☐ Most Q2's and Q3's (plus some Q4's) have reciprocal arrangements—fee-split agreements—with other firms. Usually these are specialists in similar, or overlapping, industry or functional areas. Under these arrangements, the recruiting firm actively refers to other recruiters those candidates in excess of its needs and/or obtains from other firms candidates for vacancies it cannot fill. In this sense, recruiting resembles the real estate business (see Chapter 2). Your inquiry will often be referred to another recruiter—very possibly a recruiter you had not contacted—when the first recruiter suspects he or she may be able to earn *half* of a fee. (A few recruiters understand that half of a fee is better than all of no fee.) Plugging into "reciprocals" should be an important part of your campaign. There are formal and informal organizations for you to approach. We'll cover them separately in Chapter 12 (High-Leverage Methods).

☐   Q2's and Q3's are better at these "sharing" arrangements because their fees are strictly contingent on successful "fills." Q4's will sometimes refer excess candidates as a matter of professional courtesy, but they don't face a compelling financial reason to do so, since fees are not contingent on the hire.

So, there are three categories of headhunters (Q2's, Q3's, Q4's) to approach three different ways (functional and industry specialists, and geographically). Samples of how to approach each of these are covered in Chapter 10. Basic rule: Craft the letter to match the headhunter's quadrant and specialties.

If you are an officer, a general manager (or other senior-level manager), or have income expectations that price you out of the "mid-level" area—say $75,000 or above—you'll want to make the "top-tier" executive search firms (Q4's, generally) aware of your interest and availability. The "heavyweight" generalist firms account for a greater share of top- and senior-level positions than their numbers would suggest. They are called "generalists" because they *do not* specialize in industry or functional areas, but seek a variety of senior-level assignments from many clients. This is a misnomer, however, because they are in effect "specializing" in senior-level positions. Be aware that these firms receive tidal waves of letters and resumes from "happy but antsy" high-income earners and aspirants. To approach this group, we have a special strategy (coming). Don't waste your stamps if you don't have a

serious shot at a senior-level position as an officer, general manager (or other senior-level manager). You won't be considered, you
won't get a reply, and the headhunter has a special place for your
resume.

Don't let the word *agency* in a firm's name discourage you from
contacting the firm, particularly when the firm is a specialist in
your industry or functional area. The "agency" description (required by law in a number of states) signifies only that the firm falls
under the auspices of a given state's regulatory processes.

In fact, because many "agencies" are Q2's, this group will often
do a much better job of "marketing" your services than will the
Q3's and Q4's. The firm has built a business on "marketing"
candidates and may know *precisely* which employer is looking for
someone with your credentials. And, this is exactly what you
want to happen on unsolicited contacts.

Reluctance to contact "agencies" probably stems from confusion over who pays the placement fee. "Applicant-Paid Fees"
and "APF" firms (those firms operating with applicant-paid fees)
have just about disappeared, except for a few pockets of the South,
and for blue- and "pink"-collar jobs. "APF" assignments are
anachronisms; most employers using third parties simply pass the
placement fee along to their customers as one of the costs of doing
business.

All states require that "APF" firms obtain signed contracts *in
advance* of any fee collection or responsibility on the candidate's
part. Read carefully—before signing—an "application" *any* firm
returns to you. Don't create a future liability for yourself by
agreeing to pay the fee if that's not acceptable to you. Small print
can be tricky; a few firms offer their clients fee refunds when new
hires resign early, and they may attempt to make you responsible
for the refund through tricky fine print. The legality of this may be
questionable, but don't automatically assume that an "application" or "data sheet" is innocuous. Line through and initial any

parts of the headhunter's form that is disagreeable. Be sure to retain a copy of any material you complete and return to the firm.

SEASONALITY OF THE HEADHUNTER'S PORTFOLIO

The headhunter's client assignment load—his "portfolio"—is not constant, but is subject to changing client requirements. There are two distinct headhunting "seasons" when client requirements are highest—January through March and September through mid-November. Because the headhunter's workload is more concentrated during these periods, consider timing your contact with one of them. Your chances of favorable evaluation and the financial and responsibility upgrades that follow will be higher when the recruiter is busiest and has more assignments to consider you for.

Peak season is January to March each year. New corporate budgets are in effect; major staff additions typically are planned to take effect with new budgets. The corporation also has its recruiting budget unspent and ahead of it for the year. Also, something in the corporate psyche says new hires should start early in the year.

The second busy season is September to mid-November, reacting to spring and summer attrition. Very little search work goes on during summer months: Executives and potential candidates are busy with vacations. Even headhunters like to go to the lake. Immediately following Labor Day, though, activity picks up until interrupted by November and December holidays, and "expiring" budgets. Also, at the end of the year, jobs are frequently left vacant to "get in under" salary budgets as year-end closings approach. So:

Best job-campaigning "season".................January to March

Second best...........................September to mid-November
Worst..Summer

Interesting parallel: Direct mail experts have reached similar conclusions for effectiveness of mailing campaigns:

Best general direct mail months ....January to March (Mail is read most intensely.)

Best catalog sales months...................October to November (Christmas buying.)

Worst direct mail months ....Summer (Mail isn't read; too much competition with other activities.)

SOURCES OF HEADHUNTER CONTACT INFORMATION

Locating headhunters is easier than you might think. There are inexpensive commercial sources for the data and others that will require nothing more than a little legwork.

☐ *The Recruiting & Search Report* (P.O. Box 9433, Panama City Beach, FL 32407; 904–235–3733), a newsletter and special report series for the executive search community, provides job hunters with lists of recruiters in most functional and industry specialties (including the "generalist" top-tier firms). Lists are updated three times per year; 1984 data base count was over 10,000. Write or call for pricing and availability of lists in your industry and functional areas. (Three categories—a functional list and two industries, for example—are $19.)

☐   Consultants News (17 Templeton Road, Fitzwilliam, NH, 03447; 603–585–6544) publishes *The Directory of Executive Recruiters*. The directory is cross-indexed by function and SIC and lists 2245 offices of 1341 firms in the 1984—85 edition. Price is $21 prepaid; $24 if billed. This book is available in many library reference sections as well.

☐   Order Yellow Pages directories for major cities of interest from your local telephone company at modest cost ($10 or less per city). Many headhunters will be listed, but check all possible classifications: Employment Agencies, Personnel Consultants, Executive Recruiters, and Executive Search Firms, etc. Some libraries keep Yellow Pages for remote cities; major airports usually have a big rack of them on display somewhere. Another good place to find a library of out-of-town directories is major chamber of commerce offices. Telephone the largest chamber in your area to check availability.

☐   Assemble your corporate library of trade publications, as far back as they go. Headhunters often advertise in the final three or four pages. Look through all the classified sections carefully —the headhunter may have advertised only once in the last year or so. Limited selections of trade magazines are also available in your library.

☐   Larger selections of trade magazines, particularly professional journals, are often available in the business and professional libraries of colleges and universities. Check a local college or two for available titles.

☐   Request lists of headhunters from your personal networking contacts. (But don't burden your contacts with a big typing job. A good way to do this: Ask your contact to lay all the business cards of the headhunters he or she knows on the copier and send you the copy.)

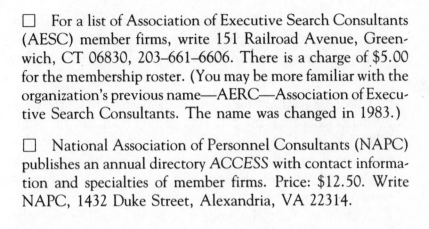

☐ For a list of Association of Executive Search Consultants (AESC) member firms, write 151 Railroad Avenue, Greenwich, CT 06830, 203-661-6606. There is a charge of $5.00 for the membership roster. (You may be more familiar with the organization's previous name—AERC—Association of Executive Search Consultants. The name was changed in 1983.)

☐ National Association of Personnel Consultants (NAPC) publishes an annual directory *ACCESS* with contact information and specialties of member firms. Price: $12.50. Write NAPC, 1432 Duke Street, Alexandria, VA 22314.

Headhunters secure with their own skills usually find no need for "high flying" titles. Be suspicious of Mr. John Jones, Esq., Executive Director, International Management Consultants, Advisers and Executive Recruiters—sounds like a Q1 to me. There *is* a relationship between high-flying titles and quality of work—it's usually inverse. Caveat emptor: J. Jones and Associates is probably the headhunter you should choose.

You'll need to assemble a list of 250–500 headhunters to maximize the effectiveness of your campaign. Sound like a lot? Remember, the average recruiter has an assignment inventory of six to eight vacancies at any one time. Mailing to them is going to be a low-percentage proposition. Because your chances with any one headhunter are slim, particularly when time is a constraint, don't hurt your chances by contacting too few.

You are interested in a "new and better" position than the one you have or the one you recently left. To obtain that position, *you must sell your way into it*, at every stage. Each step must be thoroughly planned and perfectly executed. Success in accomplishing your goal will come from the strength of your campaign, rather than your credentials.

This may or may not be a concept you are comfortable with, and you may not agree with it, particularly if you are a *credential-heavy* specialist or manager. I want to be very clear on several points:

☐   Because you have taken the initiative to contact the head-hunter (rather than the other way around), he or she will be highly skeptical. Do you recall the A and B categories? Your task here is to make *certain* you are *perceived* as an A; if the headhunter considers you a B, the game is over, and you've wasted a contact. *By definition*, most unsolicited contacts will be B candidates. Your challenge will be to outshine the other people who have contacted the headhunter.

☐   Managers consistently *overestimate* their status with head-hunters and *underestimate* the competition for the choice assign-ments. When involved in "pure" recruiting, the headhunter is being paid to be highly selective. That's how the headhunter makes a living, by picking only the "best fit" for a given position from all the candidates he can find who might be qualified. Headhunters are often more difficult to impress than potential employers. Clients expect "better" candidates from head-hunters than they hire through their own efforts.

☐   The headhunter's perception of "the market" for managers and executives at your level is going to be somewhat different from yours. His "executive market" is composed of all the mana-gers and executives at, above, and below your level that he approaches and that "find him." Particularly when the recruiter is a strong one, you may be a middling candidate, like it or not. This makes a superior approach even more important.

☐   Recruiters can be called lots of names, one of which isn't *magician* (as in being able to create a perfect position for you out of thin air when none exists). Individual headhunter assignment portfolios are small, circles of familiar clients are limited, timing of your contact can be poor.

☐   The headhunter is often an independent entrepreneur. His or her sense of urgency—as applied to you—may be minimal even if you are a temporarily available superior candidate, especially when he's busy on complicated or difficult projects where you aren't a candidate, when his bank book is fat from recent projects, or even if you contacted him on a bad day.

The *cost-effective* method of contacting a large group of head-hunters is through a *direct mail campaign*. We'll cover the complete direct mail strategy in the next chapter.

— 10 —

Direct Mail and Writing Copy

THS can't make you a direct mail expert or an English language technician, but then, these are not goals of the book. Instead, I have a simpler—and more achievable—goal: to help differentiate you from the thousands of others contacting headhunters and potential employers. Notice I *did not* list the "new and better" position as a goal of the book—that's *your* goal.

We're concentrating on identifying the proper tools, then teaching you how to use them; the size and style of house you choose to build is strictly up to you.

Let's briefly turn the tables back to your role as an evaluator of other managers' skills. If you (or any headhunter, or any other line manager) were able to *objectively* analyze the credentials of a large number of managers you were considering as potential hires for your organization—1000 or more—the spread would be wide. No surprises here. Because your first clues to the performance— what has been done in the past and potential future perform- ance—of candidates are based on *written self-descriptions*, though, truly objective analysis isn't possible. The range of performance is still wide, but it's not correlated well with what the candidate actually did (or might do in the future). Instead, the spread varies with writing skill and effort put into the documents. Still, it's all you have to go on. This is where the "first cut" of the staffing game is made.

Hiring executives and headhunters you approach in your job campaign face the same difficulty: using the only indicators of performance available—candidate self-descriptions—they make deep cuts in the numbers of unsolicited contacts. Measure this against your own experience: How many hires have you made from the unsolicited contacts that crossed your desk? Your hiring rate—even the contact followup rate (where you at least investigate the candidate in greater detail)—is probably around a percent or two.

These low-percentage success rates stem more from poorly prepared contact materials than they do from your well-developed hiring skills. Do you really believe that only 1 out of 100 potential hires measures up? Try one more mental test of the concept: If you were able to hire all of the next hundred unsolicited contacts, how many success stories would you be able to report? Even the most pessimistic hiring manager would predict success rates much higher than 1%—and that makes my point: The prevailing contact methods—cover letters, resumes, etc.—just don't relate well with performance.

Our next task in *THS* is to get the rules of this game on the table. Then, we'll show you how to beat the competition by improving the quality of that initial contact and by using the rules to your best advantage. We'll be carefully planning and crafting a direct mail campaign to use with your headhunter list; most of the techniques can be used with the list of potential employers you have developed as well.

Is there anything dishonest or underhanded about developing a superior approach? Absolutely not! Headhunters (and potential employers) *want* to be impressed with your credentials. They *want* to be responsible for (or make) successful hires. In fact, I suspect those executives best able to act on material outlined in *The Headhunter Strategy* with original and well-executed copy will outperform their personal competition. So, *THS* will help the best managers move to the head of the queue and assist firms in making better hires.

Why use direct mail, anyway? After all, that daily load of computer-generated junk isn't very effective, or is it?

Yes, it *is* effective—incredibly so. Major direct mail sellers often do quite well (thank you) on favorable response rates of 1%—one favorable reply per 100 mailed. A 2% favorable response rate is the industry rule-of-thumb success standard. A basic mailing piece costs the mailer roughly a quarter (obviously more for more complicated efforts, like thick full-color catalogs). Compare this with the cost of the typical industrial sales call, which is certainly over $100 each, with most sales taking two or three calls to consummate. In fact, AT&T says the cost of the personal sales call is approaching $200.

You could accomplish your new position goal through personal "sales calls"eventually—if you had the time and money to spend doing it. But unless you are quite unusual, the time and money available to conduct your job campaign are in short supply. Therefore, the direct mail campaign is *the* strategy of choice for contacting headhunters and potential employers. It provides the maximum *total* impact—impact as measured across the complete job search—trading off individual contact effectiveness for more contacts: maximum "reach" from the money and time you have to spend.

You'll get no argument from me that the direct mail strategy is less effective than personal contacts when examined on a contact-for-contact basis, but that's not the issue. *Reach* is the issue; a job search is a low percentage proposition. Recall that one head-hunter has only a handful of assignments at any time. Your chances with any given headhunter are small. This suggests contacting more of them rather than less. The solution, then, is the direct mail campaign, where your army of inexpensive direct mail "salesmen" will be making important initial contacts.

Direct mail's other important advantage over other means of contact is that you avoid "head games" on the initial contact. Trying to establish headhunter interest on an initial telephone call (or personal visit) puts you in the junior position in the power relationship. Believe me, the headhunter gets more practice at this than you do—and he's very good at it. Trying to beat him at his game and create a favorable impression on one telephone call doesn't work well. On the other hand, once you have caught his eye—and he has to call you to find out more—the power relationship changes to your favor. He'll be listening much harder after he has taken the trouble to contact you.

OK, we've identified the proper tool. Our direct mail campaign is designed to "pull" better than the routine mailbox stuffers you get every day. It's going to emulate personal correspondence.

Let's do it.

ORGANIZING THE CAMPAIGN

Assemble all prework and research. By now, you have the following:

1. A one-page summary of your four or five most important career accomplishments (Chapter 1).
2. A list of potential employers to approach, produced from library research (Chapter 8).

3. Optional purchased list of line managers (Chapter 8).

4. A list of headhunters assembled from various sources (Chapter 9).

Next step:

Locate a local word-processing service and make the deal to produce your series of one-page letters (your count), with envelopes. Several important considerations to remember when making this arrangement:

1. You have a major project involving 40–50 hours of word-processing time. Investigate obtaining a reduced price justified by the volume of work your project represents. You should receive better treatment than a walk-in customer with a handful of letters.

2. Chances are favorable that a local entrepreneur working from home with a PC is looking for this sort of work. With the capabilities of the latest generation of personal computers, low overhead need not suggest low-quality work, but be sure to look critically at some samples of previous work produced before turning over data entry. Be skeptical about "dot-matrix" printers; most aren't yet capable of producing the "letter quality" look of "daisy-wheel" printers favored by most manufacturers. The secretarial service should have one of the state-of-the-art machines, such as an IBM Displaywriter, Lanier, or Wang. Check the services section of local newspaper classified advertising.

3. Plan and schedule your campaign carefully. Be certain the word-processing service blocks out an adequate amount of time for your project.

4. Start with data entry (entering your employer and head-hunter lists into the computer). This can be done while you are writing letters and before you are ready to print and mail them. Starting data entry first will save you several days of waiting later.

Crafting Your Letters

Rules first:

1. Letters must be grammatically perfect.
2. Don't try to do them in one night or in one sitting.
3. Assume that you fall into the A category, and use the letter to emphasize your A status.
4. Don't bring up salary, bonus, perquisites, or other similar concerns.
5. Use your three or four strongest career accomplishments to best advantage.
6. Play the headhunter's game.
7. Customize your letters.
8. One-page limit. Use "executive size" stationery and a colorful commemorative stamp.
9. Include your business card with a personal note on it.

Writing copy—effective copy, that is—is incredibly difficult. A person earning a living writing direct mail copy is very well paid; top performers in the business earn in excess of $100,000 per year. *They* go through multiple drafts on every writing project. *They* seek independent critique. You should do the same. If possible, obtain two different kinds of help: (1) from someone who is an accomplished English language technician (for form) and (2) from a sympathetic headhunter (for substance).

You cannot afford to make foolish mistakes on this contact. Would you believe fully one-third of the correspondence I receive from job seekers contains misspelled words? One advantage of the word processed letter is that once you have removed all the bugs, they're gone forever. Ask that the secretarial service produce separate draft copies of your prospect list and your letters. Proof them yourself, then have another person proof them again.

A status must be carefully and consciously established. If you aren't able to do that, you're automatically a B—and finished.

If you have done much interviewing (of candidates and potential subordinates, that is), you are aware of a natural tendency to make a decision about the candidate in the first 5 minutes of the interview. The remainder of the interview—however long it lasts—is spent seeking confirmation of that initial decision. If you can avoid making that 5-minute decision, you are truly unusual.

Because headhunters receive wave after wave of correspondence, the attention your letter will receive is measured in seconds, not minutes. One small glitch will derail your chances—and pigeonhole you to B status.

Suggesting your status to the headhunter—that you are ready to be selected as VP-Finance, for example—nudges you to consideration at that level; *demanding* a level tells the headhunter you are wishing for it. This is a subtle technique. At the end of this chapter, I've written several letters to illustrate the suggestive technique, some ways to play the headhunter's game, and how to highlight your accomplishments. I emphatically *do not* recommend that you duplicate these and use them. Remember headhunters sense cookie-cutter approaches; start over from scratch with an original effort for better results.

Customize each letter by calling the headhunter by name, the firm by name, the specialty of the firm by its name, and so on. (See the end of this chapter for examples. Our word processing is done on an IBM Displaywriter. IBM calls a basic letter the "shell document" and customized tidbits within the letter "variables." The word processor operator you select to produce your letters will be able to explain the idiosyncrasies of a particular machine.) Your word processor operator will "merge" your variables with the shell document to produce a custom piece for each prospect; it's a little like shuffling a deck of cards.

An inquiry/introduction letter to a headhunter should look just like that; it should not look like a resume—you already know what happens to resumes. So, hold your letter to one page (everyone knows resumes are two pages). Save the resume for the follow-up—and be sure it is also word-processed (2 page limit) also.

Edit, edit, edit. Keep sentences short and crisp. Every industry/functional area has its 250 or so "buzzword" vocabulary; sprinkle a few of these through your letter for effect, but overwhelming the headhunter works against you.

Multiple drafts and independent critique of your letter are essential. Remember the goal of this letter is simple: to provide enough substance to create interest while not screening you out.

When you are sure your letter is ready, sleep on it one more night, then look at it closely the next day. You'll almost certainly have a change or two to make. Then have the letter programmed at the word processing service.

I am a proponent of "executive size" (7¼ inches x 10½ inches) stationery for initial contacts, because it stands out—but not dramatically—from the run-of-the-mill correspondence headhunters receive. But don't overdo the concept: thermoset inks give the engraved impression at less cost. 100% rag content smacks of extravagance; 25% rag is sufficient. It's a little like comparing impressions created by arriving in a BMW versus a

Rolls. You want to look successful and substantial, but conservative and circumspect, not flashy.

Include your business card, with a note on the back, short and to the point—

"Bill, I am looking forward to hearing from you."

"Jack, I am planning a trip to Cincinnati on May 15. Would you like to get together for lunch?"

"Walt, I've heard a lot about you. I am looking forward to meeting you personally."

These are examples of the "little hooks" good headhunters use to land big fish. They work equally well in reverse. I suggest making a list of a dozen or so of these, then randomly including them—with the correct name, of course—with each letter.

Business cards are frequently saved—and filed—in a different location from resumes, so this is an important part of your direct mail "package." While the card won't always be saved, when it is, you'll double your exposure with this headhunter: he may flip through card and resume files separately. Cards are easier to save than resumes, which ultimately wind up in the dumpster. That one little business card may last for years.

Use a colorful commemorative stamp on your letters instead of a mailing machine. Here's one of those tiny points where QI's drop the ball. Even though you may be tempted to save time by running the letters through the Pitney Bowes, don't. You want to avoid any suggestion of mass production.

Use a juicy felt-tip or fountain pen to sign your letters. No ball-points allowed. Executives sign letters with fountain pens.

Important, important, important. Regardless of when your letters are written or typed, *date* them on a Sunday. *Place your letters in a mailbox to be picked up Sunday afternoon.*

☐   The Sunday dating suggests you wrote it on your own—not company—time. Even though it may seem contradictory, head-hunters give high marks to loyalty. Producing "confidential" inquiries on company time smells fishy—perhaps the organiza-tion is assisting you in departing. The date of your letter is going to be noticed more often than you suspect.

☐   About 80% of all first-class mail is delivered in *2 days' travel time*. This will put most of your letters on headhunters' desks on *Tuesday—the lightest mail day of the week*. Because many of the "heavyweights" receive hundreds of resumes each week your letter may get a stronger evaluation when it arrives on a light mail day.

Remember the direct mail 2% success standard? A 2% favorable response will produce 10 nibbles from your 500 letters, but you may do considerably better if your letter was well-crafted. Expect replies to start as early as that first week. Most will probably come as telephone calls, so stay rooted by the phone for 10 days or so, if possible. Make sure others answering your phone are well-coached on how to handle inquiries in your absence. If your phone is at home, having children answering it and taking messages can be deadly. The professional atmosphere you worked so hard to nur-ture on that initial written contact can be washed away quickly. Consider having a second line installed on a temporary basis with an answering machine or a short-term arrangement with an an-swering service.

If your office phone is answered by a secretary, assistant, or co-worker, you must choose between two risky options depending on the circumstances: exposing your job campaign to your organi-zation by coaching the person answering your telephone (and thereby improving the quality of the inquiry) or risking the inquiry and preserving your present job. Of course, if you are a lame duck on "special assignment," only the inquiry is at risk, and the choice is obvious.

I would like to leave you with one more thought before you start working on your letters:

"I'd rather be a hammer than a nail."

Do you remember this line from an old song? The hammer role fits most executives better than the nail role—and you practice the hammer role in all your other business affairs. Most "popular" job-hunting advice attempts to place you in the nail role. I believe the nail role is as inappropriate for job campaigning as it is for managing your other business affairs; passive managers don't rise very high or last very long. Make your letters active; they'll work better.

Sample letters to headhunters and employers (and a few more comments) follow. Again, these letters are designed to illustrate the method; they should not be used as maps to follow. Remember, headhunters will sense cookie-cutter approaches. Effective letters will reflect your original efforts and will come out of your own head. Show your initiative, don't whine or be apologetic about the contact, and stay 100% positive in these letters. Remember, you are aiming for "A" status.

Warren R. Johnson
423 Cedar Ridge
San Antonio, TX 78543
512-678-1600 (O)
512-949-1554 (H)

Mr. Jeffrey G. Jones, CPA
Finance and Accounting Placements of Oklahoma
1550 Commerce, Suite 295
Tulsa, OK 74136

Dear Mr. Jones:

I recently learned that your firm is quite active with Oklahoma and North Texas manufacturers in the financial management area. My personal expertise is in that area (I'm also a CPA, plus I have an MBA from Ohio State).

My current firm (a medium-sized well-servicing company) was recently acquired by one of the major manufacturers. Our absentee owners, heirs of the founder, had no interest in managing the firm and decided to "cash in". The new owners have indicated very few of our management-level people will stay, once our firm is combined with their current well-servicing division.

Ironically, my accomplishments as CFO made our firm an attractive buy:

- The new costing system I designed and introduced allowed us to become highly competitive in our area. Since we knew our costs exactly, we were able to eliminate unprofitable services and concentrate on the most profitable ones. Consequently, we became least cost producer in our market.

- In three years, we improved our cash flow 27% by reducing receivables from 61 days to 37 days. This freed up enough working capital to buy out three competitors.

- ROI before I became CFO in 1978 was 17% (pretax); it's now 30%+.

I can duplicate these accomplishments elsewhere. I would imagine that small to medium manufacturers (to $100MM in sales) would be most interested in my background. Relocation is no problem.

I'll be in the office all next week and look forward to hearing from you. I also have several subordinates (each hand-picked and trained by me) I would like you to know about.

Sincerely,

Warren R. Johnson

Sample Initial Contact Letter - Q3's (Industry)

Warren R. Johnson
423 Cedar Ridge
San Antonio, TX 78543
512-678-1600 (O)
512-949-1554 (H)

March 12, 1984

Mr. Jeffrey G. Jones, Vice President
Petroleum Industry Consultants
745 Mockingbird Lane, Suite 101
Dallas, TX 75222

Dear Mr. Jones:

PIC has developed quite a reputation in the oil patch - Bob Russell tells
me you were instrumental in moving him to Central Petroleum. I would like
to know you too; chances are we can help each other - I just learned of
some industry personnel changes that might interest you.

My track record as a National Sales Manager (oil field supplies) demonstrates my exceptional sales, marketing, and administrative skills.
Here's a bit of my background:

> - After becoming National Sales Manager with Consolidated Industries,
> I turned around a demoralized sales force in six months - much to the
> disappointment of our competition. Our market share is up 10% across
> all product lines; profits are up 27% and setting new records. I
> understand the relationship between leadership and profitability.

> - My five regional sales managers and twenty-six sales people are
> back in the field where they make money. I streamlined sales admin-
> istration procedures by hiring two customer service reps at headquar-
> ters, freeing the sales force from unproductive paperwork. Sales
> calls are up 33% in three months; customer complaints have been cut
> in half. $40,000 in salaries generated over a million dollars in
> reduced claims last year.

While happy and reasonably challenged where I am, it is unlikely that I'll
be able to achieve an equity position - The President is grooming his son
to take over the business. I would consider officer-level positions with
your clients (please check with me first) if stock is a possibility. My
skills would be quickly beneficial to any firm selling workover or secondary recovery equipment or processes. I'll make a change quickly for the
right opportunity.

Please phone me at your convenience next week (week of 3/19). I have
alerted my secretary - She'll put your call right through.

Sincerely,

Warren R. Johnson

Warren R. Johnson
423 Cedar Ridge
San Antonio, TX 78543
512-678-1600 (O)
512-949-1554 (H)

March 12, 1984

Mr. Jeffrey G. Jones, CPC
Southwest Executive Personnel
745 Mockingbird Lane, Suite 101
Dallas, TX 75222

Dear Mr. Jones:

Southwest Executive Personnel's reputation has reached New York. Several
associates have mentioned your firm, and you specifically. I understand
you are well-connected with Texas manufacturers and do quality work. We
should certainly talk soon - It's very likely we can help each other.

Here's a bit of my background:

> - After becoming National Sales Manager with Consolidated Industries,
> I turned around a demoralized sales force in six months - much to the
> disappointment of our competition. Our market share is up 10% across
> all product lines; profits are up 27% and setting new records. I
> understand the relationship between leadership and profitability.
>
> - My 5 regional sales managers and 26 sales people are back in the
> field where they make money. I streamlined sales administration
> procedures by hiring two customer service reps at headquarters,
> freeing the sales force from unproductive paperwork. Sales calls are
> up 33% in three months; customer complaints have been cut in half.
> An investment of $40,000 in salaries generated over a million dollars
> in reduced claims last year.

My division doesn't fit with Consolidated's long term strategies; our
chairman recently announced that the Consumer Products Division is for
sale. I have been offered other opportunities at our Greenwich, CT
headquarters, but declined them because of my desire to work in the
consumer products area.

The timing is perfect to consider opportunities in the DFW area. Joan and
I have family and friends there and look forward to returning. Please
call me at your convenience next week (week of 3/19). I have alerted my
secretary that you will be calling - she'll put your call right through.

Sincerely,

Warren R. Johnson

Warren R. Johnson
423 Cedar Ridge
San Antonio, TX 78543
512-678-1600 (O)
512-949-1554 (H)

March 12, 1984

Mr. Jeffrey G. Jones, Senior Partner
Evans, Lawrence and Webster
One Main Place, 42nd Floor
Dallas, TX 75240

Dear Mr. Jones:

Several associates have mentioned the quality of your search work for senior managers on behalf of Southwest U.S. manufacturers. Walt Hoffman (Chmn. of Lonestar Flange) was particularly complimentary. We should know each other.

My track record demonstrates exceptional sales, marketing, leadership, and administrative skills. Here's a bit of my background:

> - After becoming National Sales Manager with Consolidated Industries, I turned around a demoralized sales force in six months - much to the disappointment of our competition. Our market share is up 10% across all product lines; profits are up 27% and setting new records. I understand the relationship between leadership and profitability.
>
> - My five regional sales managers and twenty-six sales people are back in the field where they make money. I streamlined sales administration procedures by hiring two customer service reps at headquarters, freeing the sales force from unproductive paperwork. Sales calls are up 33% in three months; customer complaints have been cut in half. An investment of $40,000 in salaries generated over a million dollars in reduced claims last year.
>
> - [You get the idea. Use this paragraph to show what you can do, how you do it, and support your claim.]

I have concluded I must look outside my present firm in order to optimize my contributions. Our President reluctantly agreed to let me consider more technologically-based organizations if I will help locate and ease the transition of a successor. We should talk soon.

Please call me at your convenience next week (week of 3/19. Please don't identify your firm; office gossip starts when the headhunter calls). My secretary has your name and will put your call right through.

Sincerely,

Warren R. Johnson

Sample "Shell" Letter to Potential Employer

January 19, 1985

¥INDIVIDUAL_NAME¥, ¥TITLE¥
¥COMPANY_NAME¥
¥STREET_ADDRESS¥
¥CITY¥, ¥STATE¥ ¥ZIP¥

Dear ¥SALUTATION¥:

I have watched with some envy the progress ¥CO_NAME¥ has made in the ¥TECH_PROCESS¥ over the past several years. Your ¥PRIMARY_CUST¥ order book must look pretty solid about now.

My personal expertise is in sales of electronic subsystems and test equipment to DOD contractors, major aerospace manufacturers, and sub contractors. I'm good at what I do - have developed excellent working relationships with DOD personnel on all the products I'm involved with. My suggestions on simplified administration procedures for labor and material escalators in our contracts have saved the taxpayers several million dollars, and earned us incentive payments well over budget.

All of that is fine, but we're running out of products to sell. The primary product line run ends next June and the company (I would rather not name my company, but you've probably guessed it) doesn't have a product ready to replace it. Rather than wait for a certain staff re-duction, I believe the timing is best right now to ask if ¥COMPANY_NAME¥ might have a place for an exceptional "hi tech" account manager.

I would like to talk with you soon to expand on this letter. Could you call me next week during a free minute? Thanks for your consideration. I look forward to hearing from you.

Sincerely,

Warren R. Johnson

Sample Word Processed Variables
(see previous letter)

The word processor will efficiently and inexpensively produce custom letters from your list of variables and the document "shell" (the basic letter before the variables are added).

Compare this list of variables to the shell document (previous letter) and the next three letters (the custom letters). For simplicity, we kept the variables in the first paragraph. Your letters could be as elaborate or simple as you choose to make them.

Letter #1
        ¥INDIVIDUAL_NAME¥ Mr. David Jesson
        ¥TITLE¥ Sr. Vice President
        ¥COMPANY_NAME¥ Consolidated Electronics Corporation
        ¥STREET_ADDRESS¥ 1 Microchip Square
        ¥CITY¥ Boise
        ¥STATE¥ ID
        ¥ZIP¥ 83704
        ¥SALUTATION¥ Mr. Jesson
        ¥CO_NAME¥ C.E.C.
        ¥TECH_PROCESS¥ C^3I area
        ¥PRIMARY_CUST¥ defense

Letter #2
        ¥INDIVIDUAL_NAME¥Mr. Ray Ponder
        ¥TITLE¥Executive Vice President
        ¥COMPANY_NAME¥General Defense Electronics
        ¥STREET_ADDRESS¥1400 Harrison Avenue
        ¥CITY¥Orlando
        ¥STATE¥FL
        ¥ZIP¥32803
        ¥SALUTATION¥Mr. Ponder
        ¥CO_NAME¥G.D.E.
        ¥TECH_PROCESS¥side-looking airborne radar design area
        ¥PRIMARY_CUST¥U.S.A.F.

Letter #3
        ¥INDIVIDUAL_NAME¥Mr. Robert E. Cochran
        ¥TITLE¥Vice President/GM
        ¥COMPANY_NAME¥Associated Avionics Incorporated
        ¥STREET_ADDRESS¥666 St. Paul Avenue
        ¥CITY¥Philadelphia
        ¥STATE¥PA
        ¥ZIP¥19082
        ¥SALUTATION¥Mr. Cochran
        ¥CO_NAME¥A.A.I.
        ¥TECH_PROCESS¥remotely piloted vehicle design area
        ¥PRIMARY_CUST¥defense contractor

Warren R. Johnson
423 Cedar Ridge
San Antonio, TX 78543
512-678-1600 (O)
512-949-1554 (H)

January 19, 1985

Mr. David Jesson, Sr. Vice President
Consolidated Electronics Corporation
1 Microchip Square
Boise, ID 83704

Dear Mr. Jesson:

I have watched with some envy the progress C.E.C. has made in the C^3I area over the past several years. Your defense order book must look pretty solid about now.

My personal expertise is in sales of electronic subsystems and test equipment to DOD contractors, major aerospace manufacturers, and sub contractors. I'm good at what I do — have developed excellent working relationships with DOD personnel on all the products I'm involved with. My suggestions on simplified administration procedures for labor and material escalators in our contracts have saved the taxpayers several million dollars, and earned us incentive payments well over budget.

All of that is fine, but we're running out of products to sell. The primary product line run ends next June and the company (I would rather not name my company, but you've probably guessed it) doesn't have a product ready to replace it. Rather than wait for a certain staff reduction, I believe the timing is best right now to ask if Consolidated Electronics Corporation might have a place for an exceptional "hi tech" account manager.

I would like to talk with you soon to expand on this letter. Could you call me next week during a free minute? Thanks for your consideration. I look forward to hearing from you.

Sincerely,

Warren R. Johnson

Warren R. Johnson
423 Cedar Ridge
San Antonio, TX 78543
512-678-1600 (O)
512-949-1554 (H)

January 19, 1985

Mr. Ray Ponder, Executive Vice President
General Defense Electronics
1400 Harrison Avenue
Orlando, FL 32803

Dear Mr. Ponder:

I have watched with some envy the progress G.D.E. has made in the
side-looking airborne radar design area over the past several years. Your
U.S.A.F. order book must look pretty solid about now.

My personal expertise is in sales of electronic subsystems and test
equipment to DOD contractors, major aerospace manufacturers, and sub
contractors. I'm good at what I do - have developed excellent working
relationships with DOD personnel on all the products I'm involved with.
My suggestions on simplified administration procedures for labor and
material escalators in our contracts have saved the taxpayers several
million dollars, and earned us incentive payments well over budget.

All of that is fine, but we're running out of products to sell. The
primary product line run ends next June and the company (I would rather
not name my company, but you've probably guessed it) doesn't have a
product ready to replace it. Rather than wait for a certain staff re-
duction, I believe the timing is best right now to ask if General Defense
Electronics might have a place for an exceptional "hi tech" account
manager.

I would like to talk with you soon to expand on this letter. Could you
call me next week during a free minute? Thanks for your consideration. I
look forward to hearing from you.

Sincerely,

Warren R. Johnson

Warren R. Johnson
423 Cedar Ridge
San Antonio, TX 78543
512-678-1600 (O)
512-949-1554 (H)

January 19, 1985

Mr. Robert E. Cochran, Vice President/GM
Associated Avionics Incorporated
666 St. Paul Avenue
Philadelphia, PA 19082

Dear Mr. Cochran:

I have watched with some envy the progress A.A.I. has made in the remotely
piloted vehicle design area over the past several years. Your defense
contractor order book must look pretty solid about now.

My personal expertise is in sales of electronic subsystems and test
equipment to DOD contractors, major aerospace manufacturers, and sub
contractors. I'm good at what I do - have developed excellent working
relationships with DOD personnel on all the products I'm involved with.
My suggestions on simplified administration procedures for labor and
material escalators in our contracts have saved the taxpayers several
million dollars, and earned us incentive payments well over budget.

All of that is fine, but we're running out of products to sell. The
primary product line run ends next June and the company (I would rather
not name my company, but you've probably guessed it) doesn't have a
product ready to replace it. Rather than wait for a certain staff re-
duction, I believe the timing is best right now to ask if Associated
Avionics Incorporated might have a place for an exceptional "hi tech"
account manager.

I would like to talk with you soon to expand on this letter. Could you
call me next week during a free minute? Thanks for your consideration. I
look forward to hearing from you.

                    Sincerely,

                    Warren R. Johnson

114

Notes to Sample Initial Contact Letters

If these letters are different from what you expected, I accomplished exactly what I set out to do: demonstrate some ways to spark interest without asking for a handout. These letters will probably look very different from the contact materials you would have written before reading *THS*. Remember, we are producing personal correspondence. *Start the dialog*; letters like thse should have your phone ringing quickly and often. If you try to accomplish *too much*—like asking to be presented to a client in that first contact—you jeopardize your standing, and risk "B" status.

The goal is to project *just enough brashness* to convince the headhunter you know exactly who you are, where you have come from, and where you are going—without stepping over the line. Approach him apologetically, whine about your company or present status, or look like thousands of unsolicited contacts: go to the end of the line.

The sample letters in this portofolio were printed on our IBM Displaywriter in "prestige elite" typeface. They should be indistinguishable from your secretary's Selectric. When programmed in the word processor, you can produce hundreds of equal quality, at low cost. Use these for inspiration. Here are some additional general guidelines and suggestions:

☐ *For all headhunter letters*: Hint (only) at industry/functional/quadrant distinctions; don't make any letter lean so hard in one direction that it could not work in another. You never know in advance what the headhunter might have in an assignment inventory, what sort of reciprocal arrangements are in place, new specialties added, and so on.

☐ If you decide to use a "reference link" (someone's name you think the recruiter will know or will be impressed to hear) in your letter, coach your contact ahead of time on how a call from the recruiter should be handled. Many recruiters will call the person mentioned in the letter before contacting you.

☐ Here's an *important* suggestion concerning references. References are not alays what they purport to be, particularly when they are checked verbally—the person you think may be an excellent reference may in reality be devastating to your chances instead. So *check your reference*. Ask a close friend to approach the reference as a "consultant" (a telephone call is fine and the "consultant" description is 100% accurate). Provide your "consultant" with a list of three or four questions to ask the reference. Get complete feedback from your "consultant" on how your reference handled the contact and whether you received good marks. Don't take the chance that your high-level contact may say something to a headhunter or hiring manager that would not be said to your face.

☐ Headhunters *live* on trade intelligence, so the good ones will quickly take the bait when you suggest you have valuable information to trade or share, particularly when the headhunter's industry and functional specialties are the same as yours, close to yours, or when he has active assignments in those areas. Recruiters are particularly interested in personnel changes that imply future third-party search work may be in order. This is how the recruiter builds and maintains an assignment portfolio and it will generate a lot of return telephone calls. (Ask in your letter for the recruiter to call you; better for him to pay for the call on the initial contact. After that, bear the expense when necessary.)

☐ *For Q2's:* Suggest in the initial contact letter that you are aware the recruiter is well-connected in your industry, function, or geographic area of interest. Because you are trying to convince headhunter to make calls to clients on your behalf, make the case that you represent a quick and easy placement. Don't overdo it; just hint. Remember, the Q2 operates by marketing candidates—the easier the placement, the better—and earns contingent fees. Since Q2's depend on unsolicited contacts, candidates are "sorted" by *ease of placement*, not necessarily by strength of credentials.

☐ *For Q3's:* Contingent search firms offer a double opportunity. Because fees are contingent on successful hires, the Q3 will often act like a Q2 (as a candidate marketer) when encountering a particularly "placeable" candidate, so the comments on Q2's apply to Q3's as well. Then, you'll also have a shot at the Q3's assignment portfolio. Recruiting stops once an attractive candidate (or two) is located and interviews for the position.

☐ *For Q4's:* A little intrigue is useful in your Q4 letters, but imitating Robert Ludlum is too heavy. Remember that Q4's are the masters of the head game—don't try to take them on directly, because you'll lose the battle—and the contact. High-level referral links work well with Q4's; but assume they will all be checked; many will. These people frequently run with the major corporation officer set; they have to—that's where the senior-level assignments come from.

☐ *For Industry Specialists:* When writing to recruiters known to be industry specialists, put some of your industry "buzzword" vocabulary to work, but do it gently. Make sure the recruiter is aware you know the ropes, but don't try to overwhelm anyone in the process. That's counterproductive. Define your industry with a broad brush; try suggesting some related areas where your experience would be relevant. Too narrow a slot to fit in limits the "universe" of opportunities where you may be considered a candidate; by defining your area of interest or specialty too narrowly, you may extend the time necessary to complete your job campaign successfully, limit your response, and waste your money.

☐ *For Geographic Approaches*: When looking to move to (or remain in) a specific area, include comments about your industry *and* functional specialties, but don't overdo industry-specific descriptions of yourself or requirements. You want a shot a diverse opportunities when relo is your first goal. Remember the *relatively* high correlation between recruiter location and assignment location.

☐ *For Potential Employers*: Potential employer letters should look much like your headhunter letters. Depending on your industry and functional specialties, you may want to develop more than one letter. Because we can't cover every contingency, we wrote one letter to demonstrate how the word processor combines a "shell' document with the "variables" you develop, then produced three custom letters. These should give you ideas on how to craft a letter to prospects. Select attractive areas in your background and relate those to the target audience.

Followup Letters and "Resumes"

Every nibble your initial mailing creates requires a followup letter. You'll be sending far fewer followups than intial contact letters, though (remember the 2% direct mail "success standard"?), so it won't be necessary to have these word processed. Each followup will be different enough to require an original effort anyway. *Don't drop this ball*; this is an important opportunity to outshine your personal competition. And, there's going to be plenty of competition for the opportunities you turn up, especially if you are a candidate at the GM or officer level.

You'll usually be asked to provide a resume to the headhunter or line manager who is interested. If you were prepared for the telephone contact when it came, you'll have a good idea of what the requested "resume" should look like. Tailor this "resume" to the interests of the recruiter or potential employer and *remember the negative side of resumes* while you are preparing it: information overload. Keep it short—one page is best—and leave more out than you put in it. Your goals are unchanged: *generate the interview and don't be screened out of consideration.*

Use the followup letter to confirm the face-to-face meeting with the headhunter or potential employer, or suggest one if you weren't able to work it into the initial conversation. Restate and emphasize the important accomplishments included in the original letter (remember *something* in that original letter sparked the interest).

Do not omit followup letters to headhunters and potential employers even if the "fit" was poor on the initial contact. Even if the "opportunity" explored wasn't promising or attractive, the recruiter may turn up something else, feedback to the client may modify the scope of the position, and so on. Manage this contact well and you'll become part of this recruiter's future candidate base. "Right of first refusal" on future assignments is too valuable a status to waste. Be sure the headhunter understands what your desires are and what it's going to take to move you.

This principle applies equally when communicating with line managers. An internal referral (with key manager sponsorship) is powerful leverage.

Sample followup letters and "resumes" to recruiters and potential employers follow. Use these as an inspiration to create your own.

Warren R. Johnson
423 Cedar Ridge
San Antonio, TX 78543
512-678-1600 (O)
512-949-1554 (H)

March 12, 1984

Mr. Jeffrey G. Jones, Senior Partner
Evans, Lawrence and Webster
One Main Place, 42nd Floor
Dallas, TX 75240

Dear Jeff:

I enjoyed our recent conversation. I am looking forward to investigating
the Vice President, Marketing & Sales position with your client in greater
detail.

Expanding on several points we discussed:

Yes, I do understand that your client's organization is somewhat larger
than my current firm and that management and leadership skills would have
to be more broadly applied. My leadership record dates back to elementary
school, and I have proven my management capabilities many times (Please
see attached resume, highlighting my leadership and management experience).

Also, in my current organization, we haven't had the "luxury" of a large
staff, so I have had to wear many hats not indicated on my resume, and
that we didn't get around to covering in our conversation.

As for compensation required to consider the position, I would prefer to
keep the subject open for the time being. Let's discuss that after I have
a more complete understanding of the job, the location (San Antonio is a
moderate cost-of-living area), and potential for growth, O.K.?

We should meet soon to continue the discussion. Are you planning to visit
San Antonio before April 7? I'll be in Dallas then and have some free
time that afternoon - Will call you Tuesday to discuss.

Sincerely,

Warren R. Johnson

encl: resume

-- Confidential --

Warren R. Johnson
423 Cedar Ridge
San Antonio, TX 78543
512-678-1600 (O)
512-949-1554 (H)

Synopsis. Johnson's twelve year performance record in the U.S. consumer products industry (health and beauty aids) demonstrates superior management skills, leadership, competitiveness, and concern for profit. This record shows conclusively that Johnson is qualified and prepared to assume officer level duties in the industry.

1972-Present - <u>Consolidated Industries Consumer Products Division</u>

1980-Present. National Sales Manager. Directed five regional sales managers and twenty-six field sales reps. Increased market share of key product lines 10% while overall industry was up only 3%. Eliminated unprofitable lines, redundant personnel, and procedures; profit improvement 1981, +12%; 1982, +17%; 1983, +27%. Effective personal/professional relationships with key decision-makers of consumer product buyers (major discounters, retail chains, and distributors).

1976-1980. Manager of National Accounts. Directed three national account representatives, personally handled K-Mart, Sears, Rite Aid accounts. Doubled Consolidated's business with the thirty-two customers in the National Accounts Program. Recruited two key sales reps from competitors. Represented the division at trade gatherings and conventions.

1972-1976. Sales Representative. Took territory rated number 15 in the organization to number 3 in 18 months. Promoted to New York metro territory, largest in the division. Extensive travel and entertaining of key buyers for major NY chains.

1968-1972. Commissioned officer and pilot, USAF. OTS Honor Graduate.

Education: BSBA, Ohio State University, 1968
           1982-83. Completed 15 semester hours graduate coursework to
           improve financial skills.

Personal: 38 years old, married 16 years (Judy), 2 children, active leader
          in community affairs (United Way, Junior Achievement, Indian
          Guides). Past/present leadership roles: Vice President College
          Fraternity; President, NY Chain Store Suppliers Assoc; many
          others.

121

Sample Followup Letter (Poor Fit) - Recruiters

Warren R. Johnson
423 Cedar Ridge
San Antonio, TX 78543
512-678-1600 (O)
512-949-1554 (H)

Mr. Jeffrey G. Jones
Evans, Lawrence and Webster
One Main Place, 42nd Floor
Dallas, TX 75240

Dear Jeff:

Thanks for the consideration for the National Sales Manager position with
your client. We agreed that the fit wasn't quite right - Your client is
interested in someone with slightly lower income expectations and who is
prepared to spend four or five years in the position.

I would rather wait for the VP Sales/Marketing position I'm qualified for
(keep me in your active file) where my contributions will be greater and
immediate.

There is someone several years behind me I believe you should approach: I
have watched Mr. Mike O'Neil, National Accounts Manager for Apex International, in action at a number of industry gatherings. He is an excellent
performer I have tried to hire myself; unfortunately, we have no place to
put him. O'Neil is certainly promotable, but is going nowhere at Apex;
their system is backed up with people. Please do not use my name when
(if) you choose to approach him.

Let's keep in touch. I'll be attending the Health and Beauty Aids Manufacturers Association convention next month in Chicago. How about lunch?

Sincerely,

Warren R. Johnson

P.S. Under separate cover, I'm sending one of those arrowheads (a bird
     point) my daughter and I found in North Carolina last summer (we have
     a dozen others) for your boy. This one is very different from the
     Plains varieties we have in Texas. I hope he ads it to his col-
     lection and enjoys it.

122

Warren R. Johnson
423 Cedar Ridge
San Antonio, TX 78543
512-678-1600 (O)
512-949-1554 (H)

Mr. David Jesson, Sr. Vice President
Consolidated Electronics Corporation
1 Microchip Square
Boise, ID 83704

Dear Mr. Jesson:

Thank you for your recent call and your taking time from your busy schedule to ask about my background. I had heard about C.E.C's new Space
Defense Division, but was not aware of the growth planned for this group.

Yes, I am a degreed engineer - BSEE (1970) from Texas A&M. Your guess of
my employer was right on the mark. Please don't talk with them yet,
though. They aren't aware that I contacted you; corporate posture at this
point is to minimize the need for sales people to look outside, but I must
do that. Once we have established some strong mutual interest, I'll be
glad to provide internal references.

Following your suggestion I will call Mr. Dave Henderson, VP/GM of the
Space Defense Division next week to schedule a meeting. And yes, my
security clearance is current.

Again, thank you for your interest.

Sincerely,

Warren R. Johnson

123

Warren R. Johnson
423 Cedar Ridge
San Antonio, TX 78543
512-678-1600 (O)
512-949-1554 (H)

Mr. Ray Ponder, Executive Vice President
General Defense Electronics
1400 Harrison Avenue
Orlando, FL   32803

Dear Mr. Ponder:

Thank you for your recent call and your taking time away from your busy
schedule to ask about my background.

At this point, I must pass on the opportunities at G.D.E. as you described
them. The account rep position would have been very interesting to me
several years ago, but I believe my skills and expertise would be more
valuable at a higher organizational level, say National Accounts Manager
or Regional Sales Manager.

Can we keep in touch? I would like to keep my credentials under consideration at G.D.E. I have a great deal of respect for what you are accomplishing with the major defense contractors and am certain I could make an
important contribution at a higher level.

Sincerely,

Warren R. Johnson

Notes to Followup Letters and "Resumes"

In the first followup letter, Johnson responded to a concern the headhunter voiced: Johnson's track record, while interesting, might be too "thin" because his experience was with a much smaller firm than the one with the assignment. So, we used the followup letter to address the concern and to try to turn it into an advantage and delay talking about compensation until the interview. Ditto for the "resume" included with the letter.

In the second followup letter (to a potential employer responding to the initial inquiry), we used the followup letter to restate and reinforce the points raised in the initial letter.

Have a goal to accomplish on each followup letter. This goal must be more definitive than simply dropping more information about yourself into the headhunter's or hiring manager's lap. Too much information will subject you to the same sort of screening treatment you worked hard to avoid in the initial contact letter.

Admittedly, you will not always have enough information to act on effectively. I still believe initiative (the "hammer role") is important in executive-level self-marketing campaigns. The keys to making this work are your listening and questioning skills, inductive reasoning ability, and your ability to present your case persuasively—and these are all qualities that headhunters, hiring managers—and you—look for in making hires.

—11—

Budgeting

Job search budgeting is another of those subjects most other writers have not taken seriously, leaving you to start from scratch or forget about. Then, it becomes one of those "loose ends" I mentioned earlier in the book that is neglected by many job seekers. That's incredible! What is more important than your own *money*? Budgeting is a critical early step in planning any project and *especially* the job search, because it's the most important limitation facing you.

Let's cover several important points up front:

1. You may have to reorganize your personal finances.
2. The job search either is important or is not. If it is important, it follows right behind food and shelter in spending priorities. If it is not important, don't waste *any* time and money on a worthless project.

3. A thorough and hard-hitting job campaign need not cause you to take out a second mortgage on your home, but it will definitely not be cheap. Be prepared—before you start—to adequately fund your job campaign. While you may decide you can't afford all the things you would *like* to do, make sure funds are available for all the things you *should* do. When properly planned and managed, the job search should reward you quickly, by paying back much more than its up-front costs.

4. The major reason small businesses fail—even those businesses with an outstanding product—is that they are under-capitalized. Your job search resembles a small business—and *you* are the product. Fail to finance the project adequately, and you'll risk wasting all money spent—then be worse off, instead of better. I'll say that again: If you underfund your job campaign, you stand to waste all the money you spent on it, then be no better off than when you started.

5. All legitimate job hunting expenses are tax deductible—The government subsidizes your job search by your tax rate. (If your tax rate is 40%, 40¢ of each dollar spent on your job search will come off your tax bill, when you itemize.) But, keep detailed records and all receipts to prepare for a possible IRS challenge. Even incidentals add up; start now with a detailed list of out-of-pocket expenses. Long-distance calls, mileage (to/from the printer, the library, the newsstand), postage, this book—don't miss anything.

6. Money isn't the only "consumable" in a job search. There are two other important but finite resources you'll want to budget: time and mental energy. Time, because you are splitting it between the job search and other responsibilities, particularly if you are still employed and your

campaign will be competing with your current employment. Mental energy, because the job search is an incredibly intense activity featuring mental highs and lows that cannot be sustained indefinitely.

Money

It's going to cost you to do it right. Exhibit 1 summarizes our earlier suggestions. I have marked essential items with an X, optional items with (O). See the notes at the end of this chapter for explanations of several line items.

By steering a "middle of the road" course—say $1600 spent on the job search—you would be out-of-pocket less than a thousand dollars, allowing for a 40% marginal tax rate. If you are a $40,000 per year manager, a 20% salary increase produced by a superior job campaign will "pay back" your out-of-pocket costs in less than two months, without counting the tax effects. Higher salary levels, larger increases, and higher marginal tax rates will pay back your job campaign even faster.

Telephone Expenses

Keep telephone expenses under control through advance planning and organization:

1. Before you call anyone over commercial lines, call 800 information first. Determine whether your party has an 800 (in-WATS) number first; many will.

2. Open an account with one of the long-distance telephone

companies competing with AT&T if you have not yet done so. This will cut your long-distance bill by 20–40%.

3. Investigate the new programs offered by AT&T. Forced to be competitive by the new long-distance carriers, AT&T is developing packages of long-distance hours that can cut your total bill significantly.

4. Don't confuse activity with results. Most telephone time is wasted. Have a goal to accomplish on every telephone call, not just a list of things to talk about.

Resist the temptation to call *anyone* collect, unless this is *volunteered*. Even if volunteered, perception of you as a substantial executive may be questioned when you call collect. It's not worth the risk.

Time

Once again it's going to cost you. I recall an article about job hunting that appeared in *The Wall Street Journal* several years ago. One of its premises was that *on the average*, an executive should be prepared to spend the same number of weeks campaigning as thousands of dollars in annual compensation expected. This is overly pessimistic—by that standard, Lee Iacocca would be pushing up daisies before he could find another job. However, be prepared to spend up to 6 months, or even more.

Any decision on which position to accept is related to personal situation and staying power. If unemployed, the position you turned down during the first week of your search looks a lot better after 6 months of fruitless spadework. If employed, you may choose to keep looking for years. Here's an interesting fact to ruminate and include in your planning: Each month you *don't* draw a salary costs you 8.3% of your annual compensation (1 year divided by 12 months equals 8.3% per month).

An important advantage of the direct mail job campaign is that it can be organized and conducted in a short time span; results will also come in quickly. Networking and employment advertising approaches stretch out longer—they include activities out of your control that cannot be accelerated. You cannot see next Sunday's *New York Times* until it is printed, for example. The interviewing process is potentially the most time-consuming component of your campaign. Three or more interviews spread over a month or 6 weeks (or more) are typical; again, timing is mostly out of your hands.

If you succeed in:

Planning and organizing your search,

Identifying the headhunters, potential employers, and advertised vacancies,

Conducting your direct mail, networking, and employment advertising approaches,

Completing the round of interviewing that produces the ideal offer,

Accepting the new position (and resigning your old one if necessary) then,

Starting work in the new assignment,

in less than 4 months, congratulate yourself on an above-average job campaign.

See Exhibit 2 for suggestions on time budgeting.

Mental Energy

You must make it last until the project is completed. Why mention this? Too many executives naively embark on job campaigns and are mentally unprepared. There will be false trails, disappointments, and pitfalls. As an "outsider," you will be subjected to cavalier treatment by personnel departments, line managers, even clerks and jerks.

Job campaigning is stressful and emotional. I can see no way to eliminate stress and mental highs and lows from the process. You must accept them in advance, then manage them as you would part of any other project.

Exhibit 1—Finances

Phase 1	Research and Preparation	Range (Low to High)	
Books	*The Headhunter Strategy*	$16	X
	Parachute, One on One	$22	X
	Economic Report of the President, Megatrends, Third Wave	0–$40	(O)
	Major metropolitan area telephone directories	0–$25	(O)

(*Economic Report of the President, Megatrends,* and *The Third Wave* should be available at the library. You'll want your own copies of *What Color is Your Parachute?* and *One on One.* Order copies of major metro area Yellow Pages from your local telephone company.)

Resume—Programming at Secretarial Service (1–2 hr @ $15–20/hr; several revisions)		$15–40	X
Headhunter contact information		0–$25	(O)
Newspaper subscriptions—3 months			
☐ National Business Employment Weekly		$32	X
☐ One of		$26–$43	X
Chicago Tribune		$25.50	(O)
New York Times		$43.03	(O)
Los Angeles Times (16 weeks)		$32.00	(O)

☐ One other major metropolitan
daily: $21—$35 (O)

(Representative samples: *Atlanta Journal/Constitution*—
$21.96—25.21 (price varies with location of subscriber);
Denver Post—$24.00; *Houston Chronicle*—$35.22
(Saturday & Sunday only).

Stationery, "executive"-size, personalized

1000 sheets, 1000 envelopes	$100—150	X
1000 business cards	$50	X
Research assistant	$0—50	(O)
Commercial mailing list	$100—300	(O)
Industry directory	$0—25	X
Telephone (long distance)	$0—25	X

Some telephoning will be necessary on all phases, but a
telephone campaign is not included in this budget.

Subtotal Phase 1	$261—878
10% contingency	$26—88
Phase 1 costs	$287—966

Phase 2 Direct Mail Campaign   Range
                                                (Low to High)

Data entry—Programming mailing list at Secretarial Service (8 hrs @ \$15−20 per hour)	\$120−160	X
Letters—Programming/entry at Secretarial Service (1 hour @ \$15−20/hr)	\$15−20	X
Letters—Customized from Secretarial Service (8 hrs. @ 15−20/hr)	\$120−160	X
Postage—500−1000 pcs. @ 20¢/pc.	\$100−200	X
Breakdown: 250−500 potential employers 250−500 headhunters		
Telephone	\$0−100	X
Subtotal Phase 2	\$355−640	
10% contingency	\$36−64	
Phase 2 Costs	\$391−704	

Phase 3 Followup Phase	Range (Low to High)	
Resumes, customized, Secretarial Service		
(4 hr @ $15–20/hr)	$60–80	X
Letters, Secretarial Service		
(100 at avg. cost of $1.50 ea.)	$150	X
Postage—100 pcs @ 20¢ ea.	$20	X
Telephone	$100–250	X
Travel		

(We haven't budgeted for personal out-of-town travel. This budget assumes potential employers will pick up the cost of out-of-town interviews.)

Remote travel assumed by potential employer	$0	
Local mileage 500 mi @ 22¢/mi	$0–110	(O)
Subtotal Phase 3	$330–610	
10% contingency	$33–61	
Phase 3 costs	$363–671	
Total costs, phases 1–3	$1041–2341	

Exhibit 2—Time

Week 1. Preliminaries. Obtain/read *THS*, *Parachute*, *One on One*, etc. Order remote newspaper subscriptions, stationery, business cards, headhunter/line manager lists. Organize personal/job search finances. Assemble previous resumes, performance reviews, evaluations. Write one-page accomplishments paper.

Week 2. Research, writing, planning. Conduct library reference section research. Locate and make arrangements with secretarial/word processing service. Begin data entry. Write headhunter and line manager "shell" letters. Complete direct mail campaign planning. Purchase stamps. Write resume, enter at secretarial service.

Week 3. Research; start mailing campaign. Newspapers begin arriving; research and answer advertising. Headhunter/subscription lists arrive; enter list data at secretarial service. Produce first letters and mail (Sunday).

Week 4. Complete mailing campaign. Continue newspaper research/replies. Produce remainder of letters and mail. First headhunter/employer replies.

Week 5. More newspaper research/letters. Majority of headhunter/employer replies. Possible interviewing.

Week 6. Interviewing. Continue newspaper research/letters.

Week 7... until conclusion, similar to week 6. The time budget does not include the networking leg, but it should fit comfortably into this schedule without disrupting the timetable.

—12—

High Leverage Methods

Leverage: Increased means of accomplishing some purpose.

You use leverage regularly in your financial affairs:

☐ When purchasing a home, the mortgage you make on the property magnifies the effect of your down payment by five times or even more.

☐ A margin account with your broker effectively doubles the amount of stock you can control; with bonds, the effect is even greater (10:1).

☐ A thousand dollars or two in a commodity account will control many thousand dollars' worth of the underlying commodity.

The techniques discussed thus far in *The Headhunter Strategy* have dealt with *improving the odds* of finding a better position by isolating headhunters most likely to be interested in you and by locating the employers that would benefit from your industry and functional expertise. And we've increased the "punch" of what you send both by carefully crafting the direct mail campaign to separate you from the flood of other unsolicited contacts.

Because leverage "stretches" the effect of the dollars you have to spend on anything, jobhunting included, you should include it in your job campaign. *Multiple views* of your background resulting from one contact are in your interest; we haven't covered any of those yet (well, OK, the "Position Wanted" ad would meet the definition, but it made more sense to cover that in the employment advertising chapter). The rest of this chapter will deal with several high-leverage approaches to your job campaign. Cheap.

Archimedes said, "Give me a lever long enough. I'll move the earth." So, reach out with a big stick.

RECIPROCAL ORGANIZATIONS AND NETWORKS

As a general rule, headhunters don't "school" very well (as fish often do). Many of the stronger independents and firms are not "joiners." They prefer to work alone, with low public profiles, and they protect assignments and candidate data jealously. However, there are a number of headhunter reciprocal organizations you may want to contact to obtain increased "travel" of your resume. They work like this: Firms pool efforts and expertise by sharing assignments and candidate data, then split fees on assignment completion when the assignment comes from one and the candidate from the other. Sounds good in theory—half a fee for the recruiter is better than all of no fee, the candidate gets more exposure, the client is able to consider more candidates and everybody benefits, right?

Maybe not. Because the best headhunters share assignments and candidates with roughly the same enthusiasm that sharks share swimmers, reciprocal organizations tend to draw the "free-lunchers" (weaker headhunters) rather than strong ones. Weaker recruiters also depend more on the "walk-in" candidates than the strong recruiters do, so some reciprocals manage only to develop a larger float of B candidates between them.

Talk about tidal waves of paperwork! Some of these organizations are awash in it. A natural candidate for computerization, you say. True, but that's expensive: hardware, software, operators, and computer time all cost; most recruiting firms are small businesses, thinly capitalized. Also, if the firm is successful, why give away half its fees on splits? Compound the problem: The "strongest weakest" firms can afford the computerized approach; the "weakest weakest" firms can afford only Xerox machines. Catch my drift?

Nevertheless, there are survivors that do share assignments and resumes. Earlier in the book, I suggested you should not worry about the *means* by which you became considered for the position and concentrate on the positions for which you are considered. So, with much to gain and very little to lose, contacting one or more of the recruiter reciprocals is in your interest.

No recommendations or rankings are attached to these listings. Make your own judgment on the ability of any headhunter, reciprocal organization, network, or "multiple listing service" to assist you. The organizations listed are survivors in the sense that they have been around for a while. There have been (past tense) others that folded quickly.

Because these networks depend on a high-volume resume "flow" to survive, many more candidates will enter the computer or paper data base than will ever find jobs through the particular system; a 1% success rate would be optimistic. On the surface, those odds appear unfavorable, but they are still higher than your chances with employment advertising. Use the "best case/worst case" test. Best case: something happens on your resume/postage investment. (Yes, you have to send a resume. This is where the computer data come from, or what is copied to share between members). Worst case: nothing happens, and your resume/ postage investment is lost. (Of course, the ultimate worst case is that your current employer finds out about your job search, then fires you. For that reason, be careful with the "paper" networks. The computerized systems guarantee confidentiality.) The roadside is littered with belly-up networks and reciprocals. Here are the ones I know that are o.o.b.; if you have been saving information on one of them in your files, you can now use the space for something else:

> Conexxions (Boston)
> Contacts (Chicago)
> International Personnel Registry, IPR (Farmington, CT)
> Jobs International (Pontiac, MI)
> Job Scan (New Orleans)
> JobNet (Portland, OR)
> Multiple Listing Opportunities (Houston)
> MSIS, Mid-South Information Systems (Cookeville, TN)
> NET, National Employment Transmittal (Englewood, CO)
> TEN, The Exchange Network (Indianapolis)

Moreover certainly others that I never heard of have died quietly. Here are the survivors we know about:

Computerized and Paper Networks

The Career Network, sponsored by Computer Search International (CSI, 1500 Sulgrave Avenue, Baltimore, MD, 21209, 301–664–1000) is the sole surviving computerized organization of independent recruiters. The Career Network operates through the facilities of The Source, a major time-sharing service. Most functional and many different industry specialties are represented among the 60-odd member firms. The Career Network's major advantage is that all Source subscribers are capable of viewing candidates and assignment data. The Source has 55,000 members; many of these are corporate subscribers of all sizes. To have your background listed on The Career Network, write CSI, mentioning your functional and industry interests. CSI will send you contact information for the nearest member firm or the industry specialist most likely to be interested in your background. Member firms earn their fees from corporate clients; there is no charge for listing your background.

National Personnel Associates (NPA, 150 Fountain Street, Grand Rapids, MI 49503, 616–459–5861) is the largest (230 members) and oldest (founded 1956) of the paper networks. NPA members actively share resumes and assignments. Write or call for the member firm nearest you. *Most industries/functional areas* are represented.

InterCity Personnel Associates (IPA, P.O. Box 2275, Appleton, WI 54911, 414–739–7788) has 155 members active in reciprocal work. IPA has many different specialties, but is *technically oriented* (EDP and engineering mostly). Write or call for a nearby member.

First International Personnel Consultants (FIPC, 1148 Hampton Hall Drive, Atlanta, GA, 404–256–2025) has 61 members, most industries/specialties. Write or call for the nearest member or specialist.

Specialized Reciprocals

First Interview (P.O. Box 7651, Marietta, GA 30065, 404–952–1058) specializes in *sales/marketing* assignments. 85 members, many different industry specialists. The corporate head-quarters will refer you to the closest member. This is an aggressive, well-run group of headhunters, specializing in S/M assignments up to $80,000 per year. Call or write.

Insurance National Search (c/o Largent Parks & Partners, Inc., Suite 402, 13601 Preston Road, Dallas, TX 75240, 214–980–0047), 25 *insurance* industry specialists. Call or write.

National Computer Associates (c/o Systems Personnel Inc., 115 West State Street, Media, PA 19063, 215–565–8880), 25 *EDP/Computer* industry specialists. Call or write.

National Association of Physician Recruiters (c/o James Russell, Inc., P.O. Box 427, Bloomington, IL 61702, 309–663–9467). 30 members, *physician* specialists. Call or write for the nearest member firm.

I suspect there are other low-profile specialized groups yet to be found. If you find any, write us; we'll include contact information in future editions of *THS*.

Franchised Operations

There are so many of these, they would be hard to list in this book. Check local telephone directories and Yellow Pages. Internal referrals vary between organizations. By franchise group, here are the specialties and strong suits:

Roth Young	Retail/Hospitality/Food/Beverage
Fox Morris	Personnel/Human Resources
Sales Consultants	Sales/Marketing
Sales World	Sales/Marketing
Robert Half	Finance/Accounting/EDP
Management Recruiters	Manufacturing/Production

Fortune	Marketing/Manufacturing
ROMAC	Finance/Accounting/EDP/Banking
Sanford Rose	Food/Beverage
Dunhill	Numerous

Registration Services

These folks seem to come and go. There's even more turnover among these firms than among headhunters if you can believe that. They aren't really headhunters at all, but more like gigantic filing cabinets. In fact, registration services promote their services to the corporate community as being competitive with third-party recruiting—corporate clients pay annual subscription fees for the privilege of reviewing resumes in the computer data base (the gigantic filing cabinet) rather than search fees. Your resume goes into the giant hopper, the computer sorts the data, personnel departments contact you. That's the theory, anyway. (Good luck.)

Computer Assisted Recruitment International (CARI, 1501 Woodfield Road, Schaumburg, IL 60195, 312–343–4995). *Engineering/EDP oriented*, but adding other functional areas. No charge to candidates for listing; send your resume.

Computerized Listings of Employment Opportunities (CLEO, 2164 West 190th Street, Torrance, CA 90504, 213–618–0200). CLEO is a division of The Copley Press, Inc., newspaper chain. They have automated the help wanted ads; read them on your PC and apply by electronic mail. *EDP/engineering oriented; primarily West Coast* positions. No charge, but no 800 or Telenet numbers, so the call is on your nickel. Call 213–618–1525 for the communications menu.

JobLine (400 West Cummings Park, Suite 2250, Woburn, MA

01801, 617–935–8877). *Boston-area* positions, most functional areas. Call or write.

Computer Science Registry (3808 Rosecran Street, Suite 387, San Diego, CA 92110, 619–569–2818). *EDP/computer science and engineering oriented.*

Career Systems Inc. (1675 Palm Beach Lakes Boulevard, West Palm Beach, FL 33401, 305–689–3337). *Most functional/industry areas.* Call or write.

Career Placement Registry Inc. (302 Swann Avenue, Alexandria, VA 22301, 800–368–3093). *Most functional/industry areas.* At last report, CPR was charging for the registration service. Call or write.

While every registration service claims national exposure, it's a safe bet that each is strongest in its own geographic area, so consider that before registering. Also, if phone calls aren't answered or if your letter comes back, understand that it took a couple of months to get *THS* into print.

— 13 —

Making It Happen

We covered a lot of ground in Chapters 1-12 of *THS*. Wheels are turning that will improve your chances with headhunters and potential employers. *This* job campaign should deliver—by *design*, rather than chance or accident—opportunities to pursue significant financial and responsibility upgrades. You should soon be feeling some nibbles on your line. As any good fisherman knows, though, getting a nibble does not mean the fish is in the boat.

This chapter is about landing big fish.

Remember the job campaigning "effectiveness rules" from Chapter 6? Here they are again:

1. Cause interviews.
2. Minimize competition.
3. Lever your efforts.
4. Increase your desirability.

You have taken important steps to accomplish these if you are using the strategies outlined earlier in *THS*. Let's set the hook.

Initial interest usually comes through telephone calls. Be prepared; have your major accomplishments page (the long one) and your resume close by:

☐   Be ready to amplify, and defend your role in each item listed in your contact letter. Remember, something in that letter was interesting enough to cause the contact. Drive those points home.

☐   Be ready to discuss accomplishments from your long list related to the ones interesting to the headhunter or line manager.

Selectively fill in the blanks, talking from your accomplishments page and resume. You'll be asked to mail a resume to the headhunter or hiring manager—but, turn the tables. "I'll be glad to put together more information about my background for you. Which areas *in my background* would you like me to expand upon?"

Listen carefully now; your reactions at this point may reinforce the contact or break it. Take notes; make certain you understand the areas important to the headhunter or line manager.

Tailor your followup letter and word processed resume to what the headhunter or line manager wants to know. A's don't have printed resumes, or *any* resumes lying around to be sent out whimsically. Now is it clear why we never printed the resume?

Search for common ground with the person on the other end of the line such as mutual acquaintances, familiarity with suppliers or customers, product lines, processes, equipment, schools you both attended, whatever. Break down the barriers.

You must ask to carry the contact to the next step—the interview. This is tough to do. Like the rookie salesman afraid to ask for the order because of fear of being turned down, you must finally face it. You won't be offered interviews—or orders—unless you ask for them. Do it in your resume cover letter if you can't do it on the telephone. But do it.

That cover letter is important. You must continue the atmosphere created in the first contact. Back to the reference section, your trade magazines, and industry contacts for research on the company, its products, performance, and prospects. (It's likely the headhunter will not reveal the client's identity on the initial contact even if you ask. Don't push too hard or you may jeopardize the contact. A good fall-back position is to ask for the *industry* of the client next, explaining you intend to do some research, which is 100% accurate.) Some of this should be fed back to the headhunter or line manager and related to your areas of interest and expertise. Do not attempt to sharpshoot their strategies or solve their problems with this letter even when problems are obvious to you. That's naive, unrealistic, and unprofessional. You simply want to prove that you have done your homework. Most of your competitors won't send even a cover letter, will provide a printed or photocopied resume, and will not bother with the company/industry research.

Involvement of a headhunter between you and the hiring manager is a valuable asset, but you must manage the contact well. Once the interviewing process is under way, produce a letter *each week* to the hiring manager, with an "open" copy to the headhunter to keep him posted on progress. On the bottom of the headhunter's copy, include a personal comment to him written in your own handwriting:

"Bill, Jack Smith mentioned they are considering a major upgrade of the Jacksonville plant. I discussed my experience in plant design—remember, I brought XYZ's plant on-line under budget and saved three months with contract labor. I'm excited about my possible involvement and have about a hundred ideas to go over with him at our next meeting. How about next weekend? I look forward to hearing from you."

Don't be flippant with these letters: there should be plenty of material to cover: confirming meetings, suggesting followup interview dates, expanding on something from the last meeting, etc. These letters have important underlying purposes completely removed from their content.

☐   To keep you ahead of the competition for the position, by emphasizing organizational skills, followup, and interest. Experience shows that most candidates won't bother and will sit back and wait for the phone to ring.

☐   To keep your name in front of the line manager. Give him plenty of opportunities to see it in print.

☐   To provide you with a measure of control over future events. Remember the "hammer versus the nail" principle.

The headhunter provides important insulation. He is capable of bringing together deals between candidates and hiring managers that could not be accomplished. Probably you will not be the only candidate in contention for the position; ask about the competition and for client feedback.

When the headhunter encourages you, consider yourself a serious contender. If a headhunter is evasive or seems to be playing games, your sun is setting. Moving on is probably the best strategy; changing the client's mind after it's made up doesn't happen often, and the recruiter probably has other candidates.

Good recruiters earn their fees by practicing "shuttle diplomacy" while serving as middlemen between the candidates and hiring managers for negotiations on titles, responsibilities, salaries, relocation packages, perquisites, and so forth. A good recruiter will know what the client is prepared to pay and will be feeling you out for what you expect. The headhunter has the market knowledge to advise both of you on the strength of respective positions—and will, of course, be providing each with feedback on the *other's* position. Remember, if the headhunter is working on a contingent basis, he/she won't earn a nickel unless the deal is made.

On the surface, this suggests contingent headhunters may attempt to "force" hires at advanced negotiation stages, but my experience shows otherwise. Good recruiters are as interested in next year as they are in next week. Other opportunities will come along if this one cannot be put together for some reason, and professional recruiters know that. Excessive pressure at the final negotiating stage from any recruiter should be met with a walk.

OFFERS

Never accept an offer on the spot. This is bad form. Hiring managers will instantly worry about possible hidden liabilities and will wonder about how much money was left on the table. Ask that any verbal offer be put in writing. Suggest a mailgram if the headhunter or hiring manager didn't think of it. All important agreement points should be spelled out: salary, bonus, unusual perks, starting date, responsibilities, title, and so forth.

Too many executives accept verbal offers, resign positions, and then find that agreements aren't agreements. Better to find out about potential problems before you are on the payroll. You also want to start squeaky clean and without any misunderstandings in your new organization.

Ask for a few days to reflect on the offer and to discuss it with your spouse. This will allow time to receive the written offer—and to insure the written offer is equal to the verbal offer. If not, act on the differences immediately.

When ready to accept the new position, ask the new employer to be prepared to put you on the payroll immediately. Your offer to an old employer for a transition period or notice may be met with a request to clean out your desk and vacate the premises, particularly if your new employer is a competitor.

Get the money going in. Once on the payroll, you'll be running on the same track with the other executives in the organization—and that means an annual 8% (or 6%, or 10%) increase. Changing jobs means adapting to a new organization, learning new systems, new political games, new rules. All of these are unknowns—and represent new risks. You should be compensated for these when you start. Only you can decide what this premium should be.

Don't expect any organization to compromise a salary administration program for one new employee. Compensating one person at a rate greater than existing management jeopardizes the salary structure of an entire organization. It's all right to push, but you must be ready to ease up. This is another place where the headhunter's contribution is valuable. The headhunter will tell you when you are pushing the limit, when you've passed it, and (perhaps) even when you aren't asking for enough.

COUNTEROFFERS

Watch out for the voice of the devil—the counteroffer from your present employer. Don't even listen.

Counteroffers are not unusual (especially if you are a key manager) in the heat of the emotions surrounding your resignation. Your firm may try to match—or even exceed—an offer from the outside. Accepting this offer—or even listening to it—isn't in your interest in any way.

☐   While they may feign shock, dismay, hurt feelings, disappointment, guilt, remorse, and all sorts of bleeding heart emotions *now*, these will change quickly to second-guessing your long-term contributions, "loyalty," and "team spirit." Accepting a counteroffer is shortsighted, because the firm will ultimately get even—on *its* terms when *you* are totally unprepared.

☐   How can you be worth more today than you were yesterday? Is looking outside the only way to cause your firm to pay you what you are worth? That doesn't sound like a place where you would want to work. Keep your eyes straight ahead and go to work for the firm ready to compensate you at market.

☐   Even if your old firm counters the offer, you will still be the same person you always were; the company will still be the same company. The reasons for making the change are rarely completely financial—and they will still be there. Remember, the new organization was willing to pay a premium for your services. Starting out at a higher level almost always implies you'll go higher.

Make the change, and don't look back. Keep relationships with important players at your old organization intact, but politely deliver the message you have decided it's best for all concerned that you move on.

Turning Down Offers

Some won't measure up. Despite the best efforts of all parties working toward the hire, not all offers are good ones. Again, keep relationships intact. A letter to principals outlining your reasons for turning down the offer—and what it would take to put it together—will help. Direct these as high in the organization as you interviewed; something good might happen. Thank the headhunter; make sure he knows where the program broke down and what it's going to take to move you. Suggest other candidates the headhunter might approach for the position; chances are very high you'll know others for whom the potential "fit" looks good. This will help to reinforce your relationship with the headhunter and improve your future chances for higher-ranking positions.

Chipping Away at Differences

Getting close to accepting, but not quite together on compensation? Here are several strategies for nibbling at those last few dollars or percentage points:

☐ Sign-on bonuses are becoming common, particularly in technical management areas. They keep salary schedules intact. Ask the headhunter to investigate the possibility of the sign-on bonus with the client. Don't ask the potential employer yourself; this looks greedy.

☐ One week's work represents 2% of a year's earnings. Starting dates (on paper) are flexible. Who says you can't be on two payrolls at once? Again, let the headhunter handle this one with the client. The insulation the headhunter provides is an important part of your squeaky clean start with a new employer.

☐ A guaranteed 6-month review can make up several percentage points, but remember this is something of a gamble: those first six months with the new employer are not likely to be highly productive for you, even under the best circumstances. You must learn new systems, procedures, personalities, and so on, and realistically won't yet be performing well enough to command an increase.

Superior Preparation

I elected not to discuss face-to-face interviewing strategies in *THS* because there are a number of fine books in print at the library. Be certain to read at least one of these when you reach the interviewing stage of your job campaign; superior preparation will pay big dividends. Your personal competitors for the position will often depend on interviewing ability alone, and may not be well coached or prepared; you will be.

Here are a few ideas on preparation I suspect you won't find elsewhere:

☐ Ask the headhunter for some basic advice on what sort of interviews you'll face, what the interests of the interviewers will be, and so on.

☐ Order a D&B report on the organization through your friendly banker. Usual charge: about $10, well worth the expense for the quality reports D&B generates.

☐ If you are interviewing with a public company, ask your broker to obtain the last 10K (the annual report to the SEC) and the last three or four 10Q's (the quarterly reports). Don't let him charge you; he owes you one. Important: 10K's include SEC-required disclosures for *corporate* officers (an important consideration if you're a candidate at the officer level). I recommend that you *do not* ask the employer for 10K's or 10Q's, even though they are often around. Many executives won't even know what they are; you may embarrass someone.

— PART 3 —

THE HEADHUNTER STRATEGY

— 14 —

Don't Believe the Management

This is the *long-term strategy* section of the book. It's not likely to be of much use today or next week. Next year, the years after that, and continuing until your retirement is a much more useful time frame. No quick fixes here.

Consider first why headhunters exist. There are two major reasons; both are explained easily in an introductory economics course (would you believe an intermediate-level economics course?).

In free-labor markets, recruiters exist because they fill an important need for the corporation. They provide staffing help for key and critical positions *more efficiently* than their counterparts within the corporate structure. More efficiently, of course, means *at less cost*. Human resource managers—who often get stuck with the recruiting expenses—may want to throw the book down in disgust at this statement, but consider this: If you (and your cousin H.R. and line managers with other organizations) were able to competitively duplicate the independent recruiting function *within your firm*, there would be no headhunters. The market doesn't support any service that doesn't justify itself. Yet head-hunters continue to exist, quite profitably, I should add. And the headhunting business is growing, not declining. We've documented the existence of 20,000 firms, and add about 50 per week to our data base. The conclusions are inescapable: The free market wouldn't allow headhunters to exist if they didn't create greater benefits than costs. If benefits were *less* than costs, fees wouldn't be sustainable and there would be no headhunters.

I'm not completely negative about personnel departments. Many of the top third-party recruiters got started as corporate ("inside") recruiters. But, recruiting *money* is on the outside. We've documented the existence of headhunters earning—yes, earning, not billing—over $300,000 per year. The best recruiters break away to become independents. And they are entrepreneurs, not bureaucrats. Bureaucrats like security; they tend to stay where they are secure.

Personnel executives are more effective with other duties than they are with recruiting. I hold labor negotiators in particularly high regard; the best of these folks save their organizations bundles. In the *cost-containment* sense, the personnel executive works long and hard to create and maintain an effective salary administration program. You have to admire the programs that keep costs down and minimize turnover—even while noticing that individual managers may be undercompensated. However, in spite of how hard the personnel department works at keeping the salary structure standardized and equitable, individual managers will continue to fall through the cracks. Enter the headhunter.

The second major reason, just as important, but a little less straightforward, involves inefficiencies of labor markets (skip the next few paragraphs if your eyes are glazing over). Corporations, particularly the big ones, are *closed systems* for managerial employees. Each firm develops written (or if not written, well understood) procedures, systems, and standards for who earns how much, who gets promoted (and who doesn't), how long an individual must stay at one level before moving to the next, and so on. Sound familiar? These systems and procedures can be fine-tuned *within* the firm, and in many firms, they are.

However, in spite of your firm's best efforts to create an equitable salary administration program, *other* organizations aren't as progressive. They reward and promote their employees at different rates. Possibly the marketing function is held in higher regard at the other company. Or the firm is staking its future on a major R&D program, wants to attract only top engineers, and is willing to *overcompensate* them as an attraction for a more risky assignment.

Headhunters trade on these differences—the "imbalances" in compensation and promotion rates between firms. To the extent that your firm undercompensates or underpromotes employees, they become targets for the headhunters' silver tongues. No, it's not illegal (A. Lincoln signed a document several years ago outlawing what you are considering). The opposite is also true. You'll attract top performers from the competition when you are willing to pay a little more or promote a little faster.

I've had line managers indignantly tell me (stuffed shirts, they) that headhunters are really capable of only one thing: ratcheting up salary levels. That's preposterous, of course. Headhunters don't set salary scales nor can they determine what an individual is "worth" to a client organization; only line managers do that. "Blaming" the headhunter for an uncompetitive salary schedule or unrecognized employee is analogous to "blaming" Sara Lee because you ate a second dessert. But, headhunters will *discover* the undercompensated marketing (engineering, manufacturing,...) staff, and clean it out. If turnover is a concern, look for the root cause; headhunters' calls stop when candidates are no longer underpaid, worth more to other organizations, or interested in looking outside.

THE HEADHUNTER AS THE THIRD PARTY

At the individual level, a long-term relationship with a proficient recruiter will *help* to insure that you are being competitively compensated and challenged when compared to other executives with comparable experience, education, responsibilities, and performance. Emphasis is on the *help*; only *you* can decide what "competitive" is. You positively cannot trust the voice of the organization. (Remember the closed system?) Third parties will provide the independent verification necessary to test it. And they accomplish something that an individual company cannot do by definition: They create a competitive system where "the market" determines what an individual is "worth." For the organization, this may seem to create turnover difficulties, but somehow the firm survives. Look to the other markets where the corporation is active—markets for products and services produced and for products and services purchased. Prices are set as compromises between buyers and sellers. Headhunters, then, help remove the inefficiencies in managerial and technical labor markets, and, in the process, at the individual level they help you get the best price for the services you have to offer a firm willing to pay you.

CORPORATE "POLICY"

I can come very close to quoting from your firm's policy manual: "It is the policy of _____ Corp. (fill in the blank) to compensate its employees at a rate equal to or greater than its competition." Sound familiar? This is corporate doubletalk. The correct translation is: "We'll pay our employees at a rate consistent with the performance level we expect from them, tolerating X% of turnover per year. We'll be careful not to pay too much; if we overcompensate, we gain little, plus we leave money on the table."

Formal and scheduled compensation review procedures are common elements of most major organization compensation plans, but as progressive as they are presented to be, they are stacked in favor of the firm, not the employee. Stinginess of a given plan is typically a function of the plan's complexity: as structure and formality of the plan increase, return to the employee decreases. That tells you something about the motivation of people writing sophisticated compensation plans, doesn't it? Don't underestimate the ability of these people to camouflage the real issues—how much you get, the rate of increase, and how often you are eligible—with high principles (reputation of the firm), promises ("We have big plans for you," "Be patient," etc.), assurances that employees *are* paid competitively (by waving around the elegant but self-serving industry salary surveys), even guilt trips ("We know your department had an excellent year, and you made—or saved—us a lot of money, but division sales were down").

The people who craft the formal compensation plans are well paid for what they do—and there is a well-recognized independent (and similarly well-paid) consulting specialty to reinforce the efforts of the firm in holding down total compensation.

Paranoid? No, just realistic. Salaries, wages, commissions, bonuses, benefits, and perquisites are *costs*. The corporation exists to produce the greatest return to its stockholders, *net of costs*. The utility it creates for its employees, neighbors, the economy, and society in general is a by-product. The corporation is under pressure to keep costs down.

The officers understand this, but won't talk about it, and may not even admit it. After all, they have first claim on compensation dollars and are paid on a very different standard from the general and midlevel management of the firm. Excluding SEC-required disclosures, try to find out how much a Senior VP earns; you'll have an arm cut off at the elbow level. Officers have performance plans *they* are measured against; keeping total compensation at or below a specified level is usually one of its major goals.

Does this sound like a diatribe? It's not intended to, nor am I suggesting that you bang the drum about it and jeopardize your standing in a fine organization. I am asking only that you *understand* what's going on.

A headhunter is the *only* person who can advise you on your status versus contemporaries from a disinterested position. How valuable is your next-door neighbor's opinion on what your house is worth? Of some value, certainly, if the house is identical to yours, and he just purchased it. Is his opinion as objective as the real estate broker's who earns a living as the third party to real estate transactions? You answer that one.

For a meaningful opinion on your "market" value, keep in touch with a recruiter who specializes in similar executives and managers. "Markets" for executive-level skills are every bit as well-defined as markets for secretaries, wide receivers, or four bedroom colonials in Westport. No way, you say? Have you talked with a recruiter specialist? Or are you hung up on the personnel department's elegant salary survey data? It pays to confirm these data with a third party.

I recommend an ongoing relationship between executive and headhunter as inexpensive insurance policies for each. The "best" headhunter to take under your wing isn't necessarily the one who recruits for you—a better choice is one with experience comparable to yours, who is roughly the same age, has a track record of successful assignment completions at and above your present responsibility level.

Cement your relationship with the headhunter by being a good contact. Your confidence will be respected and rewarded. Recruiters depend on trade contacts, both as a source of nominations and for knowledge of vacancies so that potential clients can be approached. Because a headhunter's reputation is his or her most important asset, the headhunter will not use your name without your permission. The good ones are positively paranoid about reputations, because they take years to establish and about 10 seconds to destroy.

Say, however, you don't know any headhunters, or you're unimpressed with the ones you know. Let's raise your visibility to help them "find you."

—15—

Causing Your Head
to Be Hunted

Have I convinced you that it's in your interest to develop a long-term relationship with a headhunter? If not, reread Chapters 9, 13, and 14. After that, if you're still not convinced, print a thousand copies of your resume to send to blind *WSJ* and *NYT* ads. You will find no further use for this book.

On the other hand, if you received the message and are acting on it, you'll want to diversify your portfolio by broadening your exposure to headhunters generally in addition to the one or more with whom you'll be maintaining regular contact.

Raising your visibility will cause your head to be "hunted." Headhunters will approach you more often for potential upgrades. Here are ways to do it:

1.   Become active in your trade associations and professional groups. If taking a leadership role (preferable) isn't an option, develop a close relationship with the leadership. Don't neglect the Executive Director, or other full-time manager—frequently a "deep throat" headhunters specializing in your industry or functional area will be cultivating and depending upon for nominations. These groups often produce the industry Who's Who directory. Be certain that you are in it, your listing is complete, and it reflects your current responsibilities.

2.   Ditto for convention activity. Headhunters attend the one or two important annual conventions in your industry or functional areas as faithfully as you do. They often use registration information for candidate sourcing.

3.   Write, write, write for the trade press, which encourages submissions from industry executives. Headhunters devour it. Being published serves several purposes: Your attractiveness to headhunters is partially a function of your visibility in the trade; it is also related to your demonstrated leadership abilities. Both are reinforced through professional publications. Officers and higher-level managers within your industry and functional area will also notice, increasing the probability of direct contact from them.

4.   Trade publication *editors* are also excellent *sources* for headhunters (and for other executives within the industry). This is another category to cultivate at your industry and functional gatherings.

5.   Headhunters also depend on *security analysts* and the *general business press* for nominations; there are security analysts and general business writers specializing in your functional area and industry. These folks are rumormongers and gossips. As such, they are good sources of trade in-

telligence, but keep in mind that *what you say to them* will be out on the jungle telegraph as well.

6. Don't overlook the weekly business section of your *local* (not major metropolitan) paper, particularly if you live in a popular "executive suburb." Often they'll print just about every news release sent to them. When you receive a promotion or additional responsibilities, prepare your own news release and send it to the newspaper. Headhunters subscribe to these papers (and trade publications) just to see who is being promoted. They have good memories and take notes.

7. Time permitting, civic activities are useful, particularly The United Way and Junior Achievement, which often have the backing and involvement of local bigwigs. Others to consider: political activities and your college/university alumni association.

The purpose of raising your visibility is to make it easier for headhunters to notice you. These strategies, which will need to be tailored to your specific circumstances, will make you an easier "find."

If time is of the essence—your plant has been marked for closing, you've been told to "start looking," or even if the boss told you to clean out your desk—all isn't lost. Start your program anyway. It isn't exclusive of direct contact or the direct mail campaign, and you'll be laying the groundwork for subsequent contacts.

IMPROVING YOUR CREDENTIALS

Once you are more visible, your chances of getting headhunter nibbles will be greater. Now is the time to flesh out your credentials. We can generalize a bit on several issues, particularly if you aspire to assignments at the general manager level or above:

☐   Graduate degrees, particularly MBA's, are important qualifications.

If you aspire to general management—and are not simply wishing for it or fantasizing about it—lack of the MBA will haunt you. It will very likely hold you back.

I know, I know: Every second kid coming along today has an MBA. You may have one or two of them working for you now. (Some executives say that having a Harvard MBA working for you is better than having the Harvard MBA. Don't believe it; you may soon find that you are working for him—or increasingly, her.) Your travel schedule is murderous, and there is precious little time to spend with the family already. They are too expensive, and the company only pays half of the tuition. Etcetera.

These are precisely the reasons you must make the 2-or-3 year commitment to get it behind you, particularly when VP/GM (and above) is your goal.

The MBA degree is increasingly common—over 400,000 have been awarded in the United States, 80% of them within the last 15 years. Headhunters look for them—and they look hard: It's an excellent "tiebreaker" when considering two candidates otherwise similarly qualified.

Why do they look so hard? A natural tendency of the headhunter's client is to expect more (a more qualified candidate) from the headhunter than from internal recruiting efforts. ("After all, we're paying that guy a lot of money. Make him work for it.") So, if you have that "ticket-punching" MBA degree, you'll be a step or two ahead of other candidates not so equipped.

If you were foresightful enough to earn the degree at midcareer, so much the better. Once the headhunter has found you, he'll sell harder to the client on your behalf. Midcareer MBA's say a lot about the candidate:

☐ The knowledge is fresh and is tempered with "real world" experience.

☐ The candidate who took the time to get it done is highly competitive, still willing to work hard (not burned out), and has a large measure of self-discipline.

☐ The candidate knows what is required to be considered VP/GM potential.

For candidates with purely technical backgrounds (even advanced technical degrees), the MBA degree is a major key to breaking out of the "technical ghetto," even if you have demonstrated that you can manage technical employees.

You have plenty of nontraditional (other than weekday) programs to choose from; a Chicago journalist counted 38 different weekend and night programs in the Chicago metropolitan area to earn an MBA. Other major metropolitan areas are similar: there is probably a "nontraditional" program in your own backyard.

Except for the dozen or so "top-tier" business schools (Harvard, Stanford, Chicago, Wharton, Tuck, Darden, etc.), the source of your MBA probably doesn't make much difference. In fact, most of the smaller programs use moonlighting local executives with subject expertise to teach many of the business courses. In that sense, because you'll be fed "real world" experience, smaller programs may stack up well against the major schools, which use "cloistered" academics in many courses.

The IRS recognizes educational expenses incurred for maintenance or improvement of your skills or those required by your employer as legitimate tax deductions. Therefore, the government subsidizes tuition by your tax rate, for that portion not covered by your employer. You have now run out of excuses, particularly when your peers are fully qualified. Given the choice, I—and other headhunters like me— will favor your competitors with the MBA degree.

It always comes up: "What about those schools offering "life-work" credit, no classroom attendance, and correspondence classes?" These are generally regarded as transparent, ticket-punching attempts at expediency. Test the concept yourself (you already know the answer): Which would you hire, the candidate with an MBA from a California diploma mill or the candidate with the MBA earned at night from Small State U.?

Two final points on graduate education:

1. Partially completed degrees are not useful. If you were interrupted, better to say on your resume "Completed 15 semester-hours of graduate coursework to improve financial skills" than "MBA 50% complete." Present it as an accomplishment rather than a half-completed project (which has disastrous implications).

2. If you haven't been a GM, but want to be, you will underestimate the necessity for financial skills at the GM level. Confirm this for yourself by asking a GM or two whom you know about the importance of financial and quantitative skills. If you want to be trusted to manage important amounts of company money (not just a depart-

mental expense budget) you had better know the difference between internal rate of return and net present value.

Job Changes Work for You and Against You

Headhunters regard job-hoppers with even greater disdain than employers do. Make more than one change with less than 3 years' tenure, and the headhunter will regard you suspiciously. Conversely, spend 20 years with one organization, and the headhunter may question your risk-taking ability. He or she will wonder if moving you would hurt more than help.

The ideal profile for a move: Candidate has 3 to 7 years with present firm and has been promoted at least once. Headhunters are skeptical about the manager interested in a move who has not been promoted, or promoted within the last several years. Title upgrades are weaker then promotions but a lot better than nothing. Caution: While titles are not standardized between firms (what does "Director" mean, for example?) two things are: number of people supervised/directed and compensation. The recruiter looks for steady progress in both areas as a measure of your continuing promotability. Cooking up phony titles, regardless of how impressive, won't help, if these are not accompanied by concrete figures indicating people responsibility, asset responsibility, or salary earned.

"Your" headhunter can become an important and valuable asset in managing your career development. You can also use headhunter assistance in managing turnover in your organization.

—16—

Protecting Your Organization
from Headhunters

You have worked long and hard to build a team of competent managers for your organization. *Keeping* those managers rewarded and challenged is a task every bit as important and difficult. If you are not able (or willing) to do that, someone else will be. Enter the headhunter, who will methodically strip an organization of underchallenged, undercompensated executives, if he finds the opportunity to do so. The loss of one executive often portends other losses; like the camel with its nose in the tent, the headhunter will capitalize on the situation. While you may not be comfortable with this, you cannot wish it away.

Turnover cannot be eliminated totally, because of factors you cannot control. For example, you have no control whatever over another organization's need—and what it is willing to pay—for one of your key managers. Also, regardless of how progressive your succession system may be, another firm's perception of one of your people can be quite different from yours; its offer to your manager may outstrip what you are prepared to pay. There is no question that the system is costly; managers have to be replaced, retrained, and paid more.

Turnover is fought bitterly by some organizations; it's well managed by others. Procter & Gamble has probably staffed the marketing departments of more consumer-product organizations than Harvard, Wharton, Chicago, and Stanford combined. A recent P&G "alumni association" dinner in Chicago drew several thousand "graduates," yet P&G continues to maintain a reputation as one of, if not the, top consumer product marketers in the nation. How? They hire well; new hires are trained well, rewarded, and promoted quickly; P&G recognizes that turnover supports rapid development of new marketing blood. They manage turnover well and have actually turned it into an asset.

Not everyone can be a P&G, and high levels of managerial turnover are generally undesirable. Your headhunter contacts can actually *reduce* turnover within your group if you manage them well. Here's how:

Want to know what you should be paying your regional sales manager? Ask the headhunter specializing in sales managers in your industry. Obviously, if your people are underpaid, the tree is ripe for picking. Raise the rates or be prepared to face the ultimate consequences.

While headhunters live on turnover, they account for only about half of the voluntary resignations at the executive level. This half can be reduced by keeping ongoing relationships with top recruiters in the areas of concern. Ethical recruiters will not recruit executives from client organizations. Some firms even keep a heavyweight firm or two on *annual retainer*, so that their executives will be "off limits." That smells like "protection" money, though, doesn't it? I see no way to keep all the head-hunters around on the payroll—spending the money on salaries would be a better solution. Also, you have the other half of those voluntary resignations—those not "headhunter-assisted"—to worry about.

Legal actions against specific recruiters and firms have been tried, but with little effect. I know of no instance where a judge has permitted the requested restraining order to be placed against a recruiter or a recruiting firm; I have heard that a number were sought, but denied. My recommendation is to deal with the real problem rather than a symptom.

NONCOMPETES AND NONDISCLOSURES

Noncompete agreements have some application, primarily in dis-couraging key managers from "looking"—but until you litigate one, whether it will stand in court is an open question. Judges and juries are unlikely to prevent an individual from making a living, especially when attacked by a big, bad corporation, if you didn't sue the 8 or 10 other employees who jumped before this one. If I were the employee, I would say that the form was signed under duress; it probably was, since no one in his right mind would sign one voluntarily.

Nondisclosure agreements are more effective, particularly when the manager is privy to truly sensitive technical secrets or market-ing data. However, even these frequently will not stand up in court. Patents are typically assigned separately to the corporation by technical employees and are entitled to rigorous protection. But *future* patents on products, inventions, and processes aren't as easily protectable.

Marketing data are also tough to defend, particularly on existing products and processes, where strategies soon become evident, uncovered, and public. If marketing strategy is public knowledge, what's left to protect? Execution? This is thin ice, I suspect. Consider specialized counsel for crafting and litigating "non-disclosure" and "non-compete" agreements—they are out there—and be skeptical of their value in reducing turnover. The worst-case scenario? You've lost the employee to a competitor; you have expensive legal bills, gaining nothing; you still have the problem that caused a valuable employee to leave; and all his or her associates know the cause. If a headhunter was involved. . .

So, include these points in your recruiting, retention, and succession planning:

☐ At least *some* turnover is healthy for your organization, regardless of whether it's unassisted or headhunter-assisted. Turnover creates opportunities for growth within the organization.

☐ Third-party recruiters can provide independent verification of competitive compensation systems.

☐ If your management losses are growing and headhunter-assisted, you have a serious problem (probably compensation-related, because this is where headhunters quickly capitalize) that must be dealt with decisively. Noncompetes and non-disclosures may not be effective solutions to compensation problems.

— 17 —

Conclusions

I don't want to fall into the trap of rewriting the book in the final chapter. Instead, I hope to hit a few of the major points again and include others that defied a chapter location. Here goes.

What do you think about resumes after reading *THS*? It has occurred to me the folklore surrounding resume use is a little like "The Emperor and His New Clothes." In the story, it was obvious to everyone that the emperor was not wearing anything. By now it should be obvious that resumes don't work well—I feel like the character in the back row who finally spoke up. If you aren't ready to "go cold turkey," try half of your job campaign "my" way and half "their" way. I'll report the results in future editions of *THS*.

In spite of my best efforts to explain who headhunters are and what they do, this group fits no mold exactly. Headhunters are part of the corporate system, yet they are not players (or coaches or fans). To understand their corporate clients, the character of an organization, the potential of an industry, function, process, or product, they must be educated, seasoned, and competitive.

To support themselves as specialized consultants, they must associate with the executive level that can engage them and approve their bills. Yet the recruiter works for a small firm—or even alone. You can choose to ignore them (judging from the "hangups" still reverberating in my ear, many executives do just that) or you can plug into the system and reap benefits.

Benefits at the individual level go far beyond position changes, although these are the most obvious. Headhunters will help keep you challenged and rewarded *where you are*; they can help you *reduce* turnover within your firm; they are a valuable source of trade intelligence and competitive information (some may even be able to whip you in racquetball). Ignoring them is shortsighted and dumb.

Job searching, changing, and campaigning are complex tasks. (If you disagree, you've been sleeping for the past 16 chapters.) The project will return to you roughly what you put into it. I assume that luck is essentially neutral, with good and bad canceling each other out. So, expect skimpy results from skimpy attempts.

Wishing for upgrades—significant ones, not simply company changes and dressed-up drone titles—doesn't help improve effectiveness of any job campaign or headhunter contact. *Understanding* how the game is really played and then using the rules in your favor does help.

When I wrote *The Headhunter Strategy*, I did so with the assumption that more mid to upper level managers and executives need help with job search *execution* than will ever need psychoanalysis. Your head is already together, even if you have lost a job, have been swept up in a headcount reduction, or have decided to look for a greener pasture. And, chances are *very* high one or more of those will happen to you at least once during your career. So, *THS* spends more time on information, organization, and presentation skills than other job campaigning books I've seen.

THE DECK CHAIR SHUFFLE

No job campaign can qualify you for a job "over your head." Headhunters and hiring managers—paid to cause "good hires"— earn their keep by selecting the proper person for the proper job. But, many job sekers are "screened out" for reasons irrelevant to performance and before credentials and potential are even measured. It seems to me that most other job campaigning "systems" resemble the deck chair shuffle on a sinking ship when swimming makes a lot more sense.

One attribute common to the best managers I have observed is the ability to sort out important tasks from the unimportant ones, then act on the important ones. There are too many teeny little factors affecting job campaigns to worry about. You would be eligible for retirement before you could finish cataloging all of them. It's better to act on the ones that make a difference. I think I included the important ones in *THS*.

Good luck with your job campaign. Now get going.

INDEX